CW00008116

KILOMETER ZERO

The main square in a random town, bursting with spectators. Cyclists have signed in on the stage and are getting ready to start. They're waiting in the corridor on the road for a clock to strike or maybe even for the blast from a starting gun. An intense countdown is accompanied by dramatic music. When the time to start finally comes, they lunge forward.

They're riding at a slow pace because this is a départ fictif, a start that is not quite the start just yet. They will ride in a leisurely manner for a few kilometers from the town center to an open road. Then, at an exact point, the race director's hand waving a white flag will poke through the sunroof of the car ahead of the riders. There, at KILOMETER ZERO, the race will start for real.

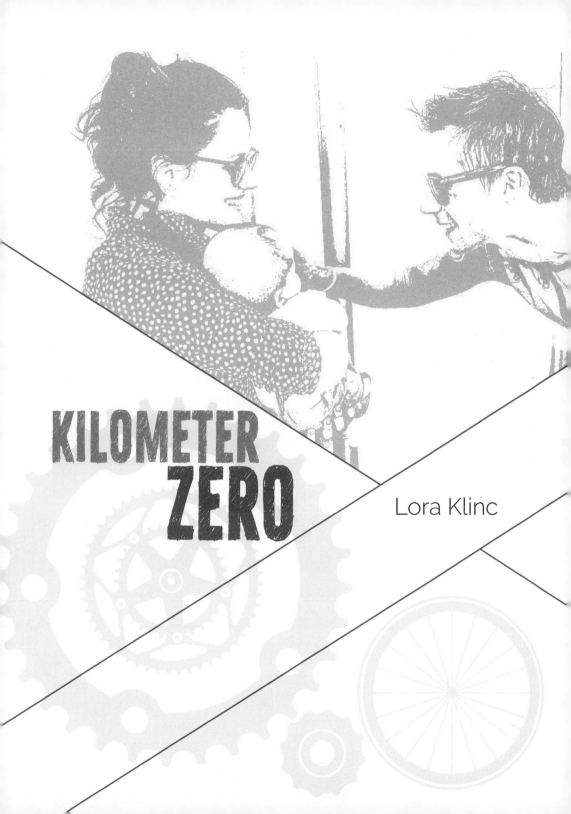

KILOMETER ZERO

Lora Klinc

For all of you who share the road with us. The fans.

Paris - Nice 2021

*I*f you are familiar with professional cycling, you are well aware I am not a man of too many words. Yet, for special people in your life you do make special exceptions.

Lora wrote this book in probably the most intense era of our lives, when, besides everything else, we were still learning how to function as a family.

When we met more than 10 years ago I was still a ski jumper. The way our paths crossed is a funny story, but let me just put it this way - all that happened while going to university ...

Coincidence? There is a lot that we could refer to as coincidence in cycling, just as much as there is in life. Sometimes things just happen because that's the way the life has to unfold.

Since then, we have ridden and covered a lot of paths together, although it was not always easy, leaving the »old life« and her own ambitions behind. Decisions, hard decisions, just finishing her master's degree with countless doors wide open, she didn't even think for a second when I asked her to risk it all and move with me to Spain for a while so I could ride a bike.

The book is unique by its composition and the information it contains. You cannot compare it to something written by journalists, writers, as it is written by the person who knows me best. Without filters and embellishments, it is written just the way things are. It's also written by the person who has witnessed my sports path from the closest perspective – the book reveals our wins, falls and sacrifices.

The way Lora explains to the reader the »regulations« and some kind of »rules« of how to follow a bike race, it is her truth. There are bound to be many who see it differently, but if you are just getting ready to step into the world of cycling, then you will likely find this kind of introduction rather interesting and fun. I would be lying if I said I wouldn't put some things differently, but then it wouldn't be her book.

Even I would like to be in our camper when it follows the races; I find the other perspective of how the race is seen so exciting. I don't have a clue when the roads close, where you find water for the camper, how to elbow with other fans to find your space at the road, nor how it is to carry around a just over two months old crying baby through the most remote hills of Spain.

She really is a woman of many talents, the best support I could ever imagine, and I am proud of her brave work. I hope you enjoy reading the book as much as we enjoy living it.

See you on the road.

Primož Roglič

Years ago one of my friends, Primož Čerin, had mentioned to me that Lora, girlfriend of Primož Roglič, really is a gifted writer; Rogla had asked him if there was any chance of getting a couple of her columns published, for others to read.

One should never overlook such signs; some of the greatest writers among us are where they are today because these signs were noticed.

By coincidence?

No, there is no such thing.

There are only things that sometimes seem to appear once in an eternity – and if you are lucky enough, you find yourself in the right place.

Lora's writing has left me speechless.

I won't try to compare her to others, she is one of a kind.

I really hoped she would keep writing, even though life with Primož put her on an enormous stage. The size of this stage is hard to comprehend for someone coming from such a small country as Slovenia. So many people desire to be in his place, in place of a boy that had to fall on his head to become a cyclist; and in place of a girl, who is always by his side, who is part of him as much as he is part of her.

The stage offers countless possibilities, and if you all of a sudden stepped under the spotlights, maybe you no longer feel the desire to write. Why would you? Writing feels so meaningless in a time when it seems that everything there is to be said, has already been said, written, explored, bought and sold. Especially, writing about things as they are and not the way they will sell, being interested in content and not giving a damn about the façade.

I said to her many times, Lora, keep writing. Your soul has been given an extraordinary gift, your heart is in it, but you are the one who has to do it. It is you who needs to write. Being gifted, if not nurtured, fades.

Once Lev was born, I feared she would no longer write. It was no longer just Primož and her, there was now someone she has to watch over even more. Someone who is above all books.

But she kept writing. And she wrote it.

This is not just a book about cycling, it is also a book about love. About dedication. A love story about two people who need each other and are devoted to one another.

Lora cheers him on. Lora follows him. Lora waits for him. Lora is terrified every time he sits on the bike, but she cannot show him her fears; she needs him to keep the immense inner force that is driving him forward.

If one were to think this is a book about cycling for dummies through eyes of a woman, they could not be more wrong.

This is a book about a love for cycling dummies through eyes of a woman.

Even if you are not a cyclist, you should read it. Cycling has the ability to sharpen your senses and, in those who are really good, sharpen their feelings. Just like with love; you need to work for it, you need to invest in it.

Primož is destined for greatness. And so is Lora. Not just by his side, on her own path too.

Some parts of this book are sheer brilliance. They got me standing on the pedals, and made me fall on the ground.

That is it. You can't train yourself to become it, you need to have it in you.

Lora is the book that is being written, just as Primož is the story that the book is written about.

They are both at the top, not just Primož.

Lora writes.

All of us, who through her writing follow the peloton trying to catch Primož, feel that there are two yellow jerseys.

One on the road and one, full of love, by his side.

Lora writes. And if everything is as it is supposed to be, she will be on large stages. What we can sense coming, is meant for the whole world to see.

All greatest things are done with love.

Primož Kališnik
Editor-in-Chief, Polet Magazine

PROLOGUE

June 2013. A hot Saturday, a perfect day for a cookout with a hot grill and a cold beer. The course of the Tour of Slovenia has meandered to the Bovec region and is just rolling over Livške Ravne[1].

I haven't the slightest idea where that is. It can't be a climb since the name of the place implies it's flat. There is no TV coverage.

Vinko is with me and we are driving a car that barely starts and we take off towards Vršič much too late. Primož and I are not a couple, although I admit I wouldn't drive to Vršič just for any friend. This is the first time I'm going to a race with a climb, because everyone knows that all the real races are supposed to be on an incline, right?

But I don't know a single thing about road cycling, except who Lance is, that there is the Tour in France, and that my dad rides a road bike. Its handlebars look like pointing downwards horns of some wild animal and its tires are so thin that next to it a cross-country ski looks as wide as a tractor tire.

Vinko reads on the internet that Primož is in the breakaway, whatever that means. They supposedly have a few minutes on those behind them. Chatter fills the car; he could win this! I don't even know who those behind them are while we're climbing the hill from the other side. And apparently there's a blue jersey from the race of Italy riding with him. I'm drawing blanks. Blue jersey? From Italy? Must be some fashion fad. Luckily we have a phone so we can read what's happening from time to time. But those were the days when coverage and data rates weren't what they are today and we have no idea that the phone bill will end up costing €350, which is an epic disaster.

The breakaway doesn't last to the end, of course, and he doesn't win, and I face a whole bunch of other stuff that makes my brow rise in ignorance by the end of the day – I'll analyze all that later. I can't ask now what's this or what's that like some airheaded bimbo.

---

[1] Ravne means flats in Slovenian.

I remember he was red as a poisonous apple and he was drinking a Coke. I gawked at that incredulously, too. But if I'd known seven years ago what I know now, I'd have probably been sitting in Kranjska Gora eating twenty-seven pizzas and drinking fourteen beers. It would have cost less than that phone bill.

But I didn't and all beginnings usually sprout from some seemingly unimportant impulse. This writing, too, grew from Sundays spent glued to the TV, answering questions such as »Hey, where do they pee then?« I like to explain these things, providing the race is not in the phase when I'm too nervous – and I don't necessarily enjoy explaining about peeing.

I love books and the freedom that words provide. A fierce attack probably has a different meaning for you than it has for me.

Cycling is a special sport. If you're adept at it or you're just coming to be, you probably know you can't compare it to anything ordinary. To anything beautiful and glossy that happens in some kind of a temporal and perhaps a spatial frame.

Cycling is freedom, and I'm not some tennis player's wife, sitting in my white frock and waving a hat from a VIP box on the Wimbledon court.

Sometimes I have to sneak up to the top of the hill, ending up with dirt behind my fingernails, sometimes I have to wash myself in a river and find large rocks to block the wheels of the camper so it doesn't careen into the valley from under my butt.

And if you're interested in how things work there and you're not as emotionally attached to all that circus as I am, you're in the right place. Understanding a bunch of guys in tights who are (most of the time) strategically stomping on their pedals in order to make it to the finish line as quickly as possible takes some intellectual effort.

Undoubtedly, you're in for something picturesque or maybe even fatal on this journey. Maybe from now on, you'll feel the same unstoppable urge to go stand at the side of the road, as the one that came over me. You can't always explain everything you do. But I know that no one is ever sent to someone purely coincidently. And that someone paid that €350 back, too.

Welcome to a world where the road is a playground.

LET IT
FINALLY BEGIN

I can't wait. We can't wait, right? The anticipation is growing and we can hardly wait for the beginning, when we'll be glued to the TV screens or road for three weeks to come. Tour of Spain is about to start. We'll get the last winner of the Grand Tour of 2019.

When they finally pile up from all over the world three days before the race, the real ceremony begins. Before such a big race as the Vuelta, they'll all go through anti-doping control. They'll shoot a few short videos and some photos for the organizers and mingle with fans, who are willing to wait for them for hours.

Then they'll train – training stays on the roster, of course. If the race starts with a shorter stage, they'll just check the final kilometers; if it starts with individual time trials, they'll ride the whole course, maybe even a few times. They'll talk to a bunch of reporters at news conferences, those who are among the top favorites in organizers' minds even at the special conference of the favorites. They'll have meeting after meeting with Sports Directors, and a day and a half before the big start they'll introduce themselves to the public on the stage in a spectacular Team Presentation.

The day before the race they are left in peace, they have only 24 hours before their world shuts down into a micro triangle road-bike-me (and other collateral conveniences and inconveniences) for 23 days.

Let's take a look at the Team Presentation for a moment. Most of those we'll meet, Primož's Team Jumbo-Visma included, are a part of UCI WorldTeam, the highest team level of road cycling in the world, and they are the best cycling teams on the planet. The cycling *Champions League* is called the WorldTour. If a team wants to make it to this elite company, it has to have a special license and at least 27 cyclists. Everything is run by the International Cycling Association, known as UCI[2].

Teams depend on sponsors and the biggest of those are mentioned in the team name. Jumbo is a supermarket chain and Visma is a software

---

[2] Union Cycliste Internationale

Tour of Spain 2019 Team Presentation

company. Of course, sponsors sometimes change, which means that the names of the teams change, too.

2016	2017	2018	2019
Team LottoNL-Jumbo (Netherlands)	Team LottoNL-Jumbo	Team LottoNL-Jumbo	Team Jumbo-Visma
Etixx-Quick Step (Belgium)	Quick-Step Floors	Quick-Step Floors	Deceuninck-Quick Step
Cannondale Pro Cycling Team (USA)	Cannondale-Drapac Pro Cycling Team	Team EF Education First-Drapac p/b Cannondale	EF Education First

Every team is based in a certain country. Teams with the highest license, so those that are part of the UCI WorldTeam, have to perform at all of the races of the UCI WorldTour[3]. But first things first.

The Tour of Spain 2019 was raced by 22 teams. All of the 18 teams then ranked in UCI WorldTeam were at the start. But 18 is not 22. Here the teams from a lower category, the so-called UCI ProTeams or professional continental teams, come into play. They are smaller in every aspect; instead of 27 riders they only need to have 14, and they are required to ride in races of lower levels, mostly in the continental races organized by the UCI. We're especially interested in those that are a part of the UCI EuropeTour.

So how did these lower level teams find themselves racing in the Tour of Spain? They get the right to compete by the organizer's invitation, in other words they are given a wild card that offers them a chance to ride in the UCI WorldTour races. A good result in any race at the highest level is a huge success for such teams[4]. Slovenia doesn't have a team in this category. We have representatives of the third quality class, continental teams[5]. No lower ranked team, i.e. third division continental team can, for example, race in the Tour de France, not even a French one. There are also development teams that offer young talented riders a chance to improve and advance. We mustn't forget that there are also women's WorldTour teams.

If you have ever seen the Team Presentation or you happen to watch one in the future, you will get an understanding about their jerseys, it will make it much easier to follow the race. Every team rides in a recognizable jersey – its colors are mostly the colors of their biggest sponsors. The trademark color of the Dutch retailer Jumbo is yellow, which makes the Jumbo-Visma riders very difficult to miss during the race, right?

---

[3] More about this later.

[4] Every single wild card team that raced in the Tour of Spain 2019 went home with a stage win.

[5] Cycling clubs Adria Mobil and Ljubljana Gusto Santic.

Jerseys change from season to season. Sometimes even in the middle of the season. Primož's team (at the time LottoNL-Jumbo) had to change their yellow jerseys for mostly black ones during the Tour de France 2018 so they would be easily distinguished from the yellow jersey of the race leader. The team also rides with uniform equipment – helmets, cycling shoes, bicycles, and everything else are sponsored.

Every team has also a so-called service course in its homeland – it's entirely possible that it's merged with the team's headquarters. And what is a service course?

> **❝** *A workshop. A fancy workshop. And a very busy warehouse. Also a kind of operational base. It is where all the bikes, spare parts and gear are kept, where the bikes are being built, inspected, and maintained. Repaired too, of course. It's stacked with rims to the roof. Every cyclist has their own box with their name and bikes and measures and settings, so the mechanics can set them up. Jerseys, helmets, shoes, everything we need. When the vehicles – cars, vans, mechanics truck, food truck, and both buses – are not being used, they're also parked in the service course. Both buses are always on the road during the racing season, be it during the races or at the training camps. In between the races they tend to park them somewhere for a few days; they don't always drive them back to the Netherlands. For example, after Tour of Valencia, they are usually parked somewhere in Spain until the Tour of Catalonia.* **❞**

Let's stay in Spain. Vuelta is one of the three biggest races of the WorldTour.

In 2019 the UCI WorldTour was comprised of 38 races all over the world. UCI WorldTeams – we'll call them the WT teams to make it easier – have to perform at all of the UCI WorldTour races. Let's just call them WT races. WT teams may also perform at all other races of the lower categories. The easiest way to remember would be the following: teams of the highest category can always race at the lower levels and teams of the lower categories can sometimes race at the higher levels, but only to a certain extent and with a special invitation.

The three biggest races are called the Grand Tour. These are the three-week races with 21 stages. The most valued amongst them is Tour de France (TDF or just »the Tour«). It carries the most points for the general classification of riders and teams, called UCI World Ranking. The overall winner of the TDF earns 1000 points. The other two Grand Tours are the Giro d'Italia, the Tour of Italy, and the Tour of Spain – Vuelta a España[6]. In 2019, my man was the number one ranked in the UCI World Ranking.

And if 23-day races (with two rest days) are the hardest, then one day races are the easiest, right? Wrong. Among one-day events, the classics are »the alpha and the omega« – prestigious races, more often than not with a very long tradition, legendary. Extremely watchable, exciting, unpredictable, thrilling.

And what is so interesting about these races that you would potentially want to spend your Easter Sunday in front of a TV rather than stuffing your mouth with ham and potica[7]? You can, of course, do both, but that is almost rocket science and you have to be well versed in these kinds of endeavors to avoid choking to death in case of sudden surprises.

Classics used to be a mystery to me (well still are a bit) as until 2020 and winning one of them, Primož would not count himself as a Classics rider, but there is something terribly romantic about them – and the fact that some are more than 100 years old only adds that sentimental note that makes the race even more attractive, if not magnetic.

---

[6] The biggest races are called Giro, Tour and Vuelta in short. Even though they all translate to a race in general – for instance Giro dell'Emilia, Tour de Provence, Vuelta a Burgos – everyone speaking the cycling language knows that the Tour is the Tour, which also goes for the Giro and the Vuelta. The Giro and Vuelta are worth 850 points each.

[7] Potica is a traditional Slovenian rolled pastry made of leavened paper-thin dough filled with any of the great variety of fillings. Walnut filling is most often used, but it can also have hazelnut, cottage cheese, tarragon, poppy seed or other fillings.

Isn't the name itself, if we take for example Strade Bianche[8], which means »the white roads«, so enticing that you just have to see how 200 of the best cyclists can make it across the dirt roads of Tuscany and after at least three bike changes slither like a huge snake out of the dust cloud, which is rising above them over the narrow cobbled ramp that leads towards the round, cobbled square Piazza del Campo in Siena old town center, where the glorious finish line awaits. One of Primož's teammates had to lay down due to exhaustion and cramps in the last corner just before the finish, despite being in the mix for the win.

The Classics can be sorted into a few groups – cobbled, Ardenne, spring, autumn, hilly – where do these names take us? Nowhere. So I'll just stop trying to pigeonhole these classics geographically and temporally into fitting groups and just let you do the classifying yourselves – if you ever feel the need to.

I'll just briefly write about the five sacred ones, the big guns – the so-called Monuments. Five of the most prestigious, longest, and oldest races that, in terms of prestige and UCI points, rank immediately behind the three Grand Tours. And that is no small feat. The winner gets 500 points[9]. Every single one of those races has special details that make them recognizable and add to their tradition.

The Italian *Milano–San Remo* is the first on the yearly calendar. The race, also known as La Primavera or La Clasicissima, was held for the first time in 1907. It's the longest among the single-day events. The 2019 edition was 291 kilometers long, and the race has come even closer to 300 kilometers quite a few times (the longest was 298 km long). It's supposed to be a sprint classic (even though many times it turns out to be quite the opposite), but, nonetheless, it's famous and recognizable because of the two climbs at the end. If you ever find yourself driving towards the French Riviera, which you

---

[8] It's been on the calendar only since 2007, but it quickly became one of the most valued races. It's mostly famous for its eleven sections of dirt road, cumulatively 63 kilometers long, on 185-kilometer race.

[9] In comparison – 500 points are also awarded to the winner of the most important one-week races – for instance the Tour of Romandie, Paris–Nice, Tirreno–Adriatico

can admire from the Autostrada dei Fiori, pay attention to the two tunnels routed under the greenhouse-coated knolls of Liguria – well, the road itself is actually one huge tunnel – especially to their names, Cipressa and Poggio. These are the two decisive climbs in the first Monument of the season.

Belgium, the cradle of road cycling. No wonder that the *Tour of Flanders*[10], held on the first Sunday in April, is a real national holiday. De Ronde has been held here since 1913 and in 2019 it was 267 kilometers long. It's known for cobblestones and short, very steep climbs. This last sentence actually epitomizes Belgian classics – cobbles, steep peaks, millions of spectators along the road with French fries and beer in their hands, and highly unpredictable weather. Koppenberg, Oude Kwaremont, and Paterberg, the last one before the finish line, are only a few of the climbs that cyclists meet on their way. You'll most probably remember the Tour of Flanders by the climb that likely doesn't decide the winner but is still very picturesque – Muur van Geraardsbergen[11]. There's a famous chapel at the top of the cobbled climb.

Muur van Geraardsbergen

---

[10] Tour de Flanders, Ronde van Vlaanderen, De Ronde.
[11] Also Kapelmur, Muur–Kapelmur.

The altitude at the top of the last climb, at Paterberg, is only 66 meters, by the way. It can't compare to the Alps, but don't let that fool you. Even though it doesn't sound like much, I seriously doubt that this climb at the end of the race in Flanders is much easier than the long alpine climbs.

The next of the greats is *Paris–Roubaix* in France. It's been around since 1896 and, with nineteen sections of *pavé*, granite cobbles, it makes for the greatest cobbled classic in the world. Maybe even the greatest classic, period. Many times held on Easter Sunday, it is about 258 kilometers long and is also known as Hell of the North, *l'enfer du Nord*. Which in a way it is.

It starts close to Paris and drags over the cobbled sections, which are known as *pavés* in cycling culture and are marked with one to five stars (luckily for the cyclists, there are only three, though often decisive, five-star sections), all the way to Roubaix, where it finishes at the velodrome. Once there, cyclists race for a lap and a half around the concrete oval. When they finish the first half of the lap, the bell rings, probably due to the French insatiable need for drama – the last lap in cycling is always announced by a bell[12]. One lap to go to eternal glory.

By the way, the finish at the velodrome has been the same from the very first rendition of the race. It was built by two manufacturers, cycling enthusiasts, who wanted the race to end at their creation. More than a century later we're still watching the April spectacle there.

But the race wasn't always so hellish. It got this reputation after World War I, which has left the roads practically non-existent due to devastation from armed conflict. The condition of the cobbled sections hasn't really changed much since – intentionally. Reportedly, one cyclist once remarked at the end of the race the state of the cobbled sections is as if someone randomly threw the

---

[12] The gentleman who must be preparing for this event the whole year round, tolls the bell so vigorously, I always half expect him to dislocate his elbow.

Dusty Paris–Roubaix

stones out of a helicopter. Namely, cobblestones are not neat cubes, arranged in lovely circles and lines such as on Prešeren Square[13]. They're 10-kilogram stones, unevenly thumped into something that aspires to be a road. The winner of the race is awarded one in the end.

Paris–Roubaix is not a special race just because of the fact that the winner is given a stone instead of a trophy, but also because the winners' names are attached to a concrete shower. Yes, you read that correctly. The legendary showers at the velodrome, which are used less and less by riders after the race, due to modern busses with bathrooms, are a monument to the winners. The rough concrete blocks, over which hang chains that open the water pipes, have golden plates adorned with the names of the winners of this agony.

And what shape are you in after finishing this race? The shaking of the handlebars leaves the palms of your hands covered in bloody blisters – despite the gloves. You probably have a puncture, a few of them. It's really great if you don't crash, but that happens quickly because your wheel gets stuck in the gaps between the cobbles. In the dry weather your mouth, nose, and eyes are full of dust. In the rain, it's not much better. It's actually much worse.

A part of this course was included in the 2018 Tour de France, when Primož rode it. After he did a recon ride over some of the cobbled sections in the spring, he merely told me in his uniquely vivid way, that your balls feel like a punching bag and your teeth clatter because your head is shaking so much you can't even see the bike in front of you, much less your power meter.

It was different later in the race. From the fortieth to the hundred and twentieth kilometer he had no water. He dropped his water bottle countless times and couldn't grab it. Because of all the shaking, his hands were numb and he couldn't let go of the handlebars – the speed was too high.

❝ *My gob was full of dust for two hours* **❞**, he blurted in his style.

---

[13] The central square in Ljubljana, the capital of Slovenia. It's named after the great Slovenian poet France Prešeren, author of *Zdravljica* (A Toast) – its seventh stanza is the Slovenian national anthem.

The oldest Monument is the Belgian *Liège–Bastogne–Liège*, the LBL or La Doyenne. The Old Lady has been around since 1892. At the end of every April finally comes the moment for all the cyclists who feel at home on hills. The LBL is a hilly classic, which was 256 kilometers long in the 2019 rendition. As the name suggests, the race starts in Liège, turns around in Bastogne and returns to Liège. The real fun begins in the second half with steep climbs back to back. The 2018 UCI Road World Champion, Alejandro Valverde, won it a whopping four times. Remember, when I said Primož is not a Classics rider? Well, he proved me wrong when he won his first Monument in 2020. As you've probably guessed, it was The Old Lady.

Let's finish, as the season finishes for many riders, with the race in Lombardy. *Il Lombardia*, which was first held in 1905, is the last of the Monuments. The biggest autumn classic often saves the best for last. It's nicknamed the Classic of the Falling Leaves[14] and is famous for favoring climbers. Held on a Saturday in October, it has been routed from Bergamo all the way to the idyllic Lake Como in the last couple of years, where it ends at the lake promenade. In 2019 it finished after 243 kilometers. Italians are the masters of spectacle and in recent years they've been persistently including the famous climbing triplets – occasionally they throw in the short San Fermo della Battaglia for a good measure, but it supposedly doesn't have any effect on the outcome.

And because the Italians do not just excel at spectacle but are also avid churchgoers, the trilogy starts with the longest of the three climbs, Ghisallo. Just before reaching the picturesque Bellagio, the chic town on the lake headland, the race makes a turn into the hills to the chapel of the Madonna del Ghisallo, the patron of cyclists, where the bikes and the equipment of the late Italian and world champions, the likes of Pantani, Coppi, Casatrelli, and others are put on display.

There's a museum of the Giro d'Italia in the newer building next door. When you enter the chapel, you shudder, but at the same time, you feel

---

[14] La classica delle foglie morte.

immense awe and respect, while inside the museum you get blinded by hundred shades of pink – both are a must-see if you find yourself in this corner of the world.

The next legendary climb is Muro di Sormano – let's pay attention to the word Muro. Namely, if you drive over Sormano on the regular road, it's nothing special. Muro means a wall in Italian, and this is definitely it. Even though it's only 1.7 kilometers long, it has gradients and words of encouragement written all over it from the beginning to the very end. The road, barely wider than a goat trail, is full of *Tifosi* (ultra-supporters) on the day of the race – Muro is their sacred place and, at the very steepest end, the gradient skyrockets to 27 percent. It is the top of the race, but likely too far from Como to decide the final outcome. The road drops from Sormano to the lake and rides along it all the way to the next climb, which is Civiglio – that's where the race has been decided in the past few years.

The three climbs of this race were also included in the Giro 2019 – with the regular Sormano instead of the wall. I doubt I will ever forget the scene with Primož hanging over the guardrail on one of the corners on the descent from Civiglio. That's Il Lombardia. It matches a vintage poster I saw, the first time I followed this race in Como, on the main square by the cathedral. The poster, inviting spectators to see the rendition back in the 1960s, shows the devil himself pulling the cyclists from the road towards the void. Above him is the chapel of Madonna del Ghisallo under an opening to heaven. Sounds familiar, right?

The races are divided into special categories, determined by the UCI rules. The new system, which came into effect with the year 2020, categorizes them from the highest to the lowest level:

> ❯ 1.UWT and 2.UWT – the highest level. UWT stands for UCI WorldTour. Number 1 marks the one-day races. Number 2 marks races that take more than one day, or stage races. For example, a one-day race classified as 1.UWT is Milano–San Remo, while Tirreno–Adriatico[15], a seven-stage race, is classified as 2.UWT.

➤ 1.PRO and 2.PRO – we know already the meaning of the number in front of the abbreviation. The code PRO replaced the code HC, which was in use up to 2020 – hors categorie, which would mean a race of special category. A 1.PRO race is for instance Giro dell'Emilia[16] and 2.PRO race in 2020 would include the Tour of Slovenia, among others.

➤ 1.1 and 2.1 – races of lower category, which are ridden mostly by the continental teams.

➤ 1.2 and 2.2 – races we can easily find close to my home. A stage race of this category is, for instance, the Istarsko Proljeće[17] and the one-day races in this category would be GP Adria Mobil and GP Kranj[18].

➤ WC and NC – WC stands for World Championship and NC stands for National Championship in cycling and sports in general. Most European countries organize their national championships on the last weekend of June, while some other countries hold their national championship already in January. In Slovenia, the time trial national championship usually takes place during Maraton Franja[19], while the road race is held at a later date.

The national champions in cycling are given a special status. The winner of the time trial or road race wears a special jersey until the next championship – usually in the colors of the national flag or with a recognizable national feature. After that, they have the right to wear the national colors on their sleeves and collar for the remainder of their careers, much like the World or European champion. And, of course, only in the discipline they have won.

---

[15] Race from the Tyrrhenian Sea to the Adriatic Sea.

[16] Italian autumn classic. In 2019 it was won by Primož Roglič. It's a one-day race and in 2019 it was 207.4 kilometers long. Its hallmark is the climb to the San Luca Cathedral above Bologna, that cyclist have to climb five times, and where the race eventually finishes.

[17] Istrian Spring Trophy, a stage race held annually in the Croatian part of the Istrian Peninsula.

[18] GP Kranj and the aforementioned GP Adria Mobil are held in Slovenia.

[19] Marathon Franja is a massive cycling event in Slovenia, held since 1982. It includes various races for riders of all levels, and a family event, and is included in the UCI Gran Fondo World Series.

Can you spot the Norwegian national champion?

With one day races explained, it's time for us to take a closer look at the stage races. These will be presented through the various happenings and mishaps that happened on the road. The Grand Tour stages are often the first-class mix of everything – some are flat, some mountainous, some are hilly, rolling, or varied, and, some are time trials – everyone can find something for themselves. Shall we begin?

START

The cyclists are ready to start. Their jerseys are fresh, the numbers attached.

The official starting list is announced a day before the start – the teams can change their riders until the very last minute. When the race starts, no further changes are allowed. Every team gets eight consecutive numbers for their riders – so from one to eight. The team leader gets the lowest number, ending in a 1. We'll never see number 99 or, for instance, 200 in the races – let's say I'm speaking just about the WT.

I hear the riders are not superstitious – save for Italians, who will turn around without hesitation and head home in the middle of a training session if a black cat crosses the road in front of them. Nevertheless, the superstition connected to the (un)lucky number 13 persists within the peloton. Riders have two numbers pinned to their jerseys on the backside, one on the left and one on the right side. The rider with number 13 will turn one of them upside down – or not, but I really can't remember the last time I saw two 13s right-side-up.

THERE'S A SAD EXCEPTION TO THIS. IN THE GIRO D'ITALIA 2011, THE BELGIAN WOUTER WEYLANDT WAS TRAGICALLY KILLED WHILE DESCENDING FROM A MOUNTAIN PASS. HE WAS WEARING THE NUMBER 108, WHICH WAS PERMANENTLY RETIRED AFTERWARD. THAT'S THE REASON WHY WE GET TO SEE THE NUMBER 109 IN THE GIRO, WHICH WE DON'T SEE IN OTHER RACES.

The organizer provides the riders with a roadbook before the start. A heavy manual with every piece of information the participants have to know about the race. They've probably seen and rode crucial parts and the profiles before. The roadbook is a real treasure trove of data about the times and locations of the stage starts and finishes, with fairly accurate timeline that tells you when the cyclists will be at certain places. There is a detailed description of the route for every stage with markings for dangerous corners, bus parking lots, the race office, and the amount of prize money, and points avaliable on top of a certain hill.

If you visit a race as a spectator, I heartily recommend you get one of those. You probably won't be so lucky as to find a hard copy, but you will surely get one on the race website. If you're a cyclist and you open it before the start, you can't help but ponder how much hard work is in front of you and inevitably almost lose the will to live. But the Garibaldi, as they call the roadbook in Italy, is a must-read for anyone who wants to win the race or just be there. Even on the side of the road.

Ladies and gentlemen, the Tour of Spain is about to begin!

L'ELIANA — 5 ETAPA — OBSERVATORIO ASTROFÍSICO DE JAVALAMBRE

170,7 km

ALTITUD	RECORRIDOS	A RECORRER	ITINERARIO	CARAVANA	34 km/h	36 km/h	38 km/h
			PROVINCIA DE VALENCIA				
			Salida neutralizada. 12:45 h.				
80	0,0	170,7	▶ Salida lanzada por la CV-375 a la altura del hito kilométrico 3 dirección La Pobla de Vallbona	11:30	12:51	12:51	12:51
90	2,3	168,4	**La Pobla de Vallbona**. Rotonda izda. CV-375	11:33	12:55	12:54	12:54
100	3,6	167,1	Rotonda dcha. dirección Benisanó CV-375	11:36	12:57	12:57	12:56
120	6,2	164,5	**Benisanó**. Rotonda izda. dirección Llíria por la CV-3692. C/ Virgen del Fundamento, badenes	11:40	13:01	13:01	13:00
150	9,0	161,7	**Llíria**. Ctra. de Valencia, Carrer del Duc de Llíria	11:45	13:06	13:06	13:05
160	9,4	161,3	Rotonda dcha. dirección Casinos por la CV-376 paso superior CV-35	11:46	13:07	13:06	13:05
160	11,2	159,5	Cruce rotonda izda. dirección Alcublas por la CV-339	11:49	13:10	13:09	13:08
470	25,8	144,9	Rotonda pasa a ser la CV-245. Comienza puerto	12:14	13:36	13:34	13:31
750	31,7	139,0	**PUERTO DE ALCUBLAS**	12:22	13:46	13:43	13:41
760	33,9	136,8	Cruce izda. C/ de la Serranía, badenes	12:25	13:50	13:47	13:44
760	34,5	136,2	Giro dcha. C/ Albufera, CV-245	12:26	13:51	13:48	13:45
725	35,0	135,7	**Alcublas**. C/ San Antonio Abad, Plaza Santa Cruz. CV-245	12:27	13:52	13:49	13:46
810	37,3	133,4	Cruce izda. dirección Bejís por la CV-235	12:30	13:56	13:53	13:49
960	42,0	128,7	**PROVINCIA DE CASTELLÓN**. CV-235	12:37	14:05	14:01	13:57
1.000	43,9	126,8	Sacañet (Ext.). CV-235	12:40	14:08	14:04	14:00
690	52,0	118,7	Cruce izda. dirección Bejís por la CV-236	12:56	14:22	14:17	14:13
770	53,8	116,9	**Bejís**. Rotonda dcha. dirección Torás CV-236	12:59	14:25	14:20	14:15
850	57,5	113,2	Torás (Ext.). Cruce izda. dirección Barracas por la CV-239	13:15	14:32	14:26	14:21
860	57,8	112,9	Giro dcha. dirección Barracas CV-239	13:16	14:33	14:27	14:22
910	59,5	111,2	Cruce izda. dirección El Toro, ctra. rural (estrecha)	13:18	14:36	14:30	14:24
915	61,5	109,2	Giro dcha. dirección Barracas por ctra. rural	13:20	14:39	14:33	14:28
990	68,0	102,7	Cruce dcha. dirección Teruel por la CV-240	13:28	14:51	14:44	14:38
985	68,4	102,3	Cruce izda. dirección Teruel por la N-234	13:31	14:51	14:45	14:39
920	69,0	101,7	**Barracas**. N-234	13:32	14:52	14:46	14:39
940	71,8	98,9	**PROVINCIA DE TERUEL**. N-234	13:37	14:57	14:50	14:44
935	74,0	96,7	🗑 N-234. Recogida de residuos	13:41	15:01	14:54	14:47
930	79,0	91,7	**Venta del Aire**. N-234	13:50	15:10	15:02	14:55
930	80,4	90,3	Cruce dcha. dirección Olba por la TE-V-2001	13:51	15:12	15:05	14:57
715	90,0	80,7	**Los Villanuevas**. TE-V-2001	14:07	15:29	15:21	15:13
690	91,0	79,7	Los Pertegaces (Ext.). TE-V-2001	14:08	15:31	15:22	15:14
680	93,8	76,9	Cruce izda. dirección Fuentes de Rubielos por la A-232. Comienza puerto	14:10	15:36	15:27	15:19
1.000	98,6	72,1	**ALTO FUENTE DE RUBIELOS**	14:10	15:45	15:35	15:26
990	99,1	71,6	**Fuentes de Rubielos**. Rotonda giro izda. dirección Teruel por la A-232	14:15	15:45	15:36	15:27
860	104,0	66,7	Cruce izda. dirección Teruel por la A-1515	14:23	15:54	15:44	15:35
870	104,6	66,1	**Rubielos de Mora**. A-1515	14:25	15:55	15:45	15:36
930	120,4	50,3	Cruce izda. dirección Albentosa N-234	15:02	16:23	16:11	16:01
930	120,7	50,0	**Venta del Aire**. Cruce dcha. dirección Albentosa por TE-V-3005	15:03	16:24	16:12	16:01
945	121,6	49,1	Cruce izda. dirección Albentosa A-6005	15:03	16:25	16:13	16:03
940	124,5	46,2	**Albentosa**. Paso en descenso con curvas pronunciadas (precaución). A-6005	15:08	16:30	16:18	16:07
890	125,0	45,7	Puente estrecho (precaución). A-6005	15:09	16:31	16:19	16:08
990	127,0	43,7	Cruce izda. dirección Manzanera por la A-1514	15:10	16:35	16:22	16:11
975	135,0	35,7	Ⓢ MANZANERA. A-1514	15:22	16:49	16:36	16:24
1.025	138,5	32,2	**Los Cerezos**. A-1514	15:38	16:55	16:41	16:29
1.120	143,0	27,7	**Fuente del Gavilán**. A-1514	15:43	17:03	16:49	16:36
1.335	149,0	21,7	Torrijas (Ext.). A-1514	15:45	17:13	16:59	16:46
1.300	150,7	20,0	🗑 Recogida de residuos	15:48	17:16	17:02	16:48
1.060	158,8	11,9	**Arcos de las Salinas**. Cruce dcha. dirección Observatorio Astrofísico por ctra. rural, paso estrecho por la población	16:02	17:31	17:15	17:01
1.080	159,6	11,1	Comienza puerto	16:13	17:32	17:17	17:03
1.950	170,7	0,0	**ALTO DE JAVALAMBRE, OBSERVATORIO ASTROFÍSICO DE JAVALAMBRE**. META	16:31	17:52	17:35	17:20

PUERTOS DE MONTAÑA

PUERTO DE ALCUBLAS
Km 31,7. Desnivel 280 m.
Ascenso 5,9 km. Porcentaje 4,7%

ALTO FUENTE DE RUBIELOS
Km 98,6. Desnivel 320 m.
Ascenso 4,8 km. Porcentaje 5,7%

ALTO DE JAVALAMBRE
Km 170,7. Desnivel 870 m.
Ascenso 11,1 km. Porcentaje 7,8%

PARADA TÉCNICA CARAVANA

BEJÍS
Km 53,8. Salida 13:09 h.

RUBIELOS DE MORA
Km 104,6. Salida 14:35 h.

MANZANERA
Km 135. Salida 15:32 h.

ARCOS DE LAS SALINAS
Km 158,8. Salida 16:12 h.

⚠ PASO CON PRECAUCIÓN BANDERAS AMARILLAS

RD-RI-R = Rtda., B = Badenes, SC = Setos, M = Medianas, GD = Curvas y cruces a la derecha, GI = Curvas y cruces a la izquierda, PE = Paso estrecho, T = Túnel

RI 1,2 - R 1,7 - RI 2,3 - RD 3,6 - RD 4,6 - R 5,6 - R 5,5 - RI 5,9 -B 6,2 - R 7 - R 7,6 - RD 7,8 - RI 8,3 - R 9,1 - RD 9,4 - R 10,1 - RD 10,6 - RI 11,2 - R 12,2 - R 25,8 - B 33 - GI 33,9 - GD 34,5 -GD 34 - GI 37,3 - GI 52 - RD 53,8 - GI 57,5 -GD 57,8 - GI 59,5 - GD 61,5 - GD 66 - GI 68,4 - RI 69,1 - GD 80,4 - GI 90,6 - PE 92,3 - GI 93,5 - GI 93,8 - RI 99,1 - GI 104 - B 104,6 -R 119,4 - R 119,7 - GI 120,4 - GD 120,7 - GI 121,6 - GD 124,5 - PE 124,6 - PE 125 - GI 127 - B 136,3 - CD 158,7- PE 158,8

STAGE ONE

AUGUST 24, 2019

SALINAS DE TORREVIEJA ·······▶ TORREVIEJA

13.4 KM TTT

UNBELIEVABLE, BUT TRUE: ROGLIČ'S FIRST STAGE SPOILED BY WATER FROM AN INFLATABLE POOL

[…] The Tour of Spain is off to a bad start for Primož Roglič. His Team Jumbo-Visma slipped on the wet road on one of the corners in the **team time trial** at Torrevieja and four riders found themselves hitting the road. They finished 40 seconds behind the fastest team, Astana.

The unforeseeable incident happened in the middle of the 13.4 km long trial. Four of the cyclists at the head of a Dutch train fell in a fairly gentle left turn, among them Roglič and Steven Kruijswijk, who finished third in this year's edition of the Tour. They were able to continue the race and didn't suffer major injuries, but they lost quite a few precious seconds. The Slovenian ace crossed the finish line with torn bib shorts on his left hip and a visible road rash. […] **The red jersey** was taken by Miguel Angel Lopez. […] (RTV MMC, 2019a)

COL	1.	LOPEZ MORENO, MIGUEL ANGEL (ASTANA PRO)	0:14:51
ITA	2.	CATALDO, DARIO (ASTANA PRO)	S.T.
DEN	3.	FUGLSANG, JAKOB (ASTANA PRO)	S.T.
SLO	99.	ROGLIČ, PRIMOŽ (JUMBO-VISMA)	+40

old on a second. Stop. What the hell is a team time trial? And if there is a team trial then there must also be a non-team, let's say an individual one?

Yep, there is. I think it's best we deal with one cyclist for starters.

Many times the stage races begin with a time trial – a race against the clock where the cyclist rides alone and the victory goes to the fastest one. The cyclists start in one-minute intervals and, commonly, the starting intervals of the first ten in the general classification are spaced even further apart. Namely, if there is no time trial scheduled in the first stage, there already is a general classification, which means that cyclists start in the opposite order – the last one in the general classification starts first. If there is no general classification, sports directors randomly divide their riders into groups.

If the first, introductory stage is a time trial, and it's shorter than eight kilometers, it's called a prologue. If it's longer than eight kilometers, it's simply called a time trial. You most commonly see the abbreviation ITT, an individual time trial.

Usually, the prologues are very short, compelling races held in historical or cosmopolitan centers so they attract a lot of spectators – the Giro prologues have started in Jerusalem, Apeldoorn in Holland, the Tour in German Düsseldorf, etc.

We can assume that organizers use the individual time trial to showcase riders, and it's also the moment when someone must be put into the leader's jersey.

You might remember the double Slovenian win in the Tour de Romandie in 2019, when Jan Tratnik and Primož Roglič finished the stage not even a whole second apart. That prologue, held in Neuchâtel in Switzerland was only 3.87 kilometers long.

In the opening time trial of Tour de France 2017 in Düsseldorf, Primož flew out of the corner in the pouring rain. Those measly 14 kilometers were very long for us.

Maybe you remember the time trial in Giro in 2019 up the San Luca climb in Bologna, where Primož won and took the lead in the general classification and therefore, the pink jersey. That was the first pink jersey for Slovenia.

Pink seems quite an unusual color for a sport like cycling, right? Pink, yellow, and red[20] are the most popular colors among the contenders for the general classification.

The yellow jersey[21] is worn by the leader of the Tour de France and, if he manages to hold on to it all the way to Paris, the traditional finish of the Tour, it's the highest accomplishment that any rider can achieve in his career. Red is reminiscent of Spanish bullfighting and is, as you probably already know, worn by the leader of the Tour of Spain, while the pink jersey is worn by the fastest rider in the Tour of Italy. The yellow and pink jerseys have a similar history. Both colors are an homage to newspapers – at the very beginning, the sponsor of the Tour de France was L'Auto, which later changed its name to L'Equipe. It was printed on yellow paper. The Italian *maglia rosa* took its pink color from the famous sports newspaper La Gazzetta dello Sport.

Let's redirect our attention away from old newspapers and back to the race. How can it be that the Tour of France starts in Germany? Surely there is no logic behind this? Well, there actually is, however it only happens during the three Grand Tours.

When a race veers off into another country, the goal is mainly the popularization of cycling – and money. The town or city hosting the *grand départ* in the Tour, or the *grande partenza* in the Giro, the grand start, to put it plainly, has to pay a few million Euros. But the money is quickly paid back by spectators over the race opening weekend. Just imagine all the hungry and thirsty cycling lovers who also have to sleep somewhere.

---

[20] Listed in the order the races are held during the season.
[21] *Maillot jaune* in French.

Recon ride before the team time trial

And at last – let's ride. A time trial is a reflection of aerodynamics, of as little air resistance as possible, and it requires special equipment. Skinsuits, tailored to these special requirements, are made of faster materials, and mostly with long sleeves because the fabric is smoother than skin. Helmets, overshoes, water bottles, and of course the bike, they're all aerodynamic. The bikes have special handlebars that allow riders to lean on their forearms to maintain as low and as aerodynamic position as possible.

Every rider is followed by a team car with at least mechanic and sports director. The rider has an earpiece with a radio connection to that car. Most of the time, the connection goes both ways[22] – the rider can always press a button and call the car if he needs a drink or information, while he can hear the sports director through the crackling in the earpiece. When riding a time trial, the connection is one-way only. You probably assumed correctly that only those in the car can speak – not just because of the connection, but also because a rider exerting himself to the very limits probably can't. A time trial is a bloody difficult feat and, when your heart rate is at 190, surviving – and not falling off the bike – is the most

---

[22] But hold on – when the cyclists ride for a national team, e.g. in the Olympic Games or World Championships, such connections are forbidden. So the unpredictable becomes down right chaotic!

Sports director giving directions to his riders from the team vehicle

important thing. The team car has a spare bike on the roof. The mechanic is in the car in case of technical problems, falls, or other reasons that would lead to the bike change.

The sports director[23] follows the rider and gives him directions over the radio – he lets him know about upcoming corners, roundabouts, potential obstacles, when the climbs are about to start, and he also provides encouragement. Information about the condition of the road and the course are of vital importance because the best of the riders try to maintain an aerodynamic position as much as possible and don't raise their heads very often – they stare at the road in front of them and try to ride the course by heart.

Due to the TV coverage of bigger races, there's a motorbike with a cameraman in front of the rider, and almost always another motorbike in charge of safety and clearing the road ahead. It's not rare that people cross the road at the least appropriate moment.

---

[23] Since we now have some knowledge about cycling, let's call him the *directeur sportif* or simply DS.

When time trialing, the riders aren't allowed to draft behind the motorcycle (they aren't allowed to do that in any circumstances during the race, but we'll talk about that later) or the rider in front of them; good time trialists namely sometimes catch riders who started the race before them. Time trials differ in length and profiles. They can be completely flat and straight, mountainous, they can have a finish climb, or they can climb from start to finish; they can be diverse (ups and downs), they can vary in technical difficulty - include, corners, roundabouts, and cobblestones, and so on.

So, how did we start the Tour of Spain? With a crash, true, but with a team time trial, in fact.

At the stage announcement at the very beginning, there is the abbreviation TTT. This means team time trial. The simplest way to put it: the entire team, all riders, in skinsuits and riding time trial bikes. They ride in a line, the first one taking the pull while the others are drafting. Every rider is at the front for a limited amount of time. It's a tactic agreed within the team; the front rider leads for as long as he can at that moment. The riders rotate at the front, while those behind try to draft as much as possible. The rider who finishes at the front veers off left or right, depending on the agreement, and the hardest work is taken over by the second in the line.

Up to a few years ago, a team time trial was still featured at the World Championship. The title of the world champion was not given to the country but rather to the cycling team. The teams wanted something in return for their riders competing for national teams with their team equipment.

In the three-week races, the team must start with eight riders[24], at shorter stage (one-week) races with one less, i.e. seven. At least four riders must cross the finish line together in the team time trials. The time is set by the fourth rider crossing the line.

---

[24] Up to a few years ago the teams started with nine riders.

This is why the team leaders, who are aiming to top the general classification[25], have to finish the time trial in that group of at least four riders. Sometimes they all finish together, which reflects the similar form the riders are in. The result is acknowledged for all eight riders. The riders who've fallen behind and cross the finish line later get their own, individual time, which counts for the general classification. If the TTT is on the first day of a stage race, the leader's jersey is taken by the rider of the winning team, who crossed the finish line first.

Let's take a look at the Team Jumbo-Visma's results on the first day of the race.

18	**Team Jumbo-Visma**	15:31	0:40	**51.815**
	ROGLIČ Primož			
	MARTIN Tony			
	BENNETT George			
	KRUIJSWIJK Steven			
	GESINK Robert			
	HOFSTEDE Lennard +3:42			
	POWLESS Neilson +3:42			
	KUSS Sepp +4:06			

They took 18th place among 22 teams, which is nothing to write home about. The first five riders, from Primož to Robert, crossed the line after 15 minutes and 31 seconds, 40 seconds behind the winning team.

These five riders were now trailing 40 seconds behind the leader of the general classification. Lennard, Neilson, and Sepp crossed the finish line later, so they were 3:42 and 4:06 behind the leader of the GC respectively. The first five members of Jumbo-Visma rode the time trial with an average speed of nearly 52 km/h.

---

[25] General classification is often simply called GC.

THE DRAMA AT THE SALT WORKS

Hoče, Saturday evening, the end of August 2019

As if by some dark magic, it was raining cats and dogs on the highway from Ljubljana to Maribor. At home, things settled down as we prepared for the highlight of the late summer. It's no secret that Team Jubmo-Visma is the favorite. They won the first TTT in the Emirates, in the Tirreno they took second place with a mere seven seconds' lag, not to mention they won the team time trial in the Tour de France. So, no excuses!

And then, I admit, I had a mild heart attack. From the dramatic start among the knolls of piled salt in the salt works, my most vivid memory of that day is the scene of something yellow, well, quite a few yellow things, flying through the air. I feel like the house imploded on the inside and only the frame is somehow left standing. After the calamity in the Giro, where we went to lift the winner's trophy and ended up with the podium place, that to us felt like winning, one would expect we've already run out of bad luck for this year. With sickness and crashes, it was a big achievement.

But no, dammit! Spain has different plans and is laughing at us on the very first day. The team was mowed down by a wet road. Many of us were completely gobsmacked. They fell like dominoes, Primož slipping first. He's sliding on his back, under the fence covering his head with his hands and protecting his face so he doesn't get his teeth smashed. Better said, he already got a good knock on his teeth. Big time!

But where did the water come from? There will be talks about conspiracy. And why was it there? Did he make a mistake? Did they screw up choosing wrong tires? I saw the flag in front of the water, yes, but they couldn't possibly see it. I'm having a tirade in front of the TV, explaining to everybody that this is a first-rate fuckup. The favorites get thrown out of the curve, puh-lease, what a farce! Why, goddammit, can't he do something easier, for instance sell bread in a bakery?

Battle wounds

Then, I calm down, stare blankly ahead for a moment, and come to the conclusion that they managed to get quite a solid result after that debacle. Pardon me, who am I kidding? The result is shit of epic proportions, and the time difference between them and the winners could be in minutes, not just seconds. Who won anyway? It could have easily happened they wouldn't have managed to get four able riders out from under that pile of twisted fence. What a shitfest that would've been!

Footage from the sport director's car later revealed that they were shocked and rattled, but they kept yelling into the radio that the riders should ride on when Primož got up, with five or even four riders.

The Jumbos then darted ahead like headless chickens and even managed to coalesce into some sort of formation, but what was going through their heads while they were, all battered and bruised, trying to patch back together their last goal of the end of season, we'll probably never know.

Maybe 40 seconds isn't that much. Yet it's also not negligible and it probably means they can't afford any more slip-ups in the race. But the words I want to utter to lift the spirits in the living room, if nothing else, don't want to come out of my mouth, because I know that something is bound to go wrong in three weeks, even if you're just sitting at home.

Chances of something going wrong get considerably higher if you're one of 176 riders who find themselves in all sorts of encounters on a 3,500-kilometer race across Spain, be it with each other, the weather, terrain, spectators, and most times with oneself. I'm wondering why he is always destined to walk arduous paths. And I'm sad. His elbow, wrist, and hip are covered in bloody road rash.

I hope the call comes as late as possible, so I can come up with a monologue that will, on a psychoanalytical level, patch up and smooth out the bumps that landing on the hard concrete imprinted in his confidence. And hope – hope has to stay alive until the very end, for as long as he can sit on his bike. Damn, this is hard.

I also hope that, when I pick up the phone, I'll hear something like: **"**It's nothing, I didn't really hurt myself, I'll win tomorrow and be back on track.**"** *But there was only the echo of silence.*

Spit out something smart, woman, quickly, come on! Why didn't I write down what I'd been mulling over earlier and what really seemed to make sense? I thought it would do. I still thought he could win the Vuelta. But instead of that he just mumbled from fucking salty Alicante something like, **"** This really isn't for me.**"** *Silence.*

" Whoosh, the front wheel went, we flew all over the place, I didn't even hit the brakes, still in position, it just threw me off. It ripped the bike off the pedals and that was that. The guys behind fell like dominoes. This cycling, it's just not for me. It's not for me.**"**

I can see him stubbornly shaking his head. **"** I'm not cut out for this, I'm really not. **"**

He hit my nerve so much that I saw red for a second and lost it, really lost my shit, and that was the best thing Primož could have done in that moment. I'm hurling Rocky Balboa's words at him, repeating the old stories of how he already proved the impossible. I'm dragging out the skeletons of historic heroes from forgotten nooks and crannies, and trying to convince him this is just the beginning and it will all fall into position in the end – and he'll be at his rightful place.

I conclude dramatically with a swearing fest, presenting myself as the main victim, saying how I will no longer be able to breastfeed because cycling is wrecking my nerves anyway and, most importantly, how he has

to believe, because he's the only one capable of doing something like that. All those sacrifices weren't in vain! I go on with a sermon about years of deprivation and woes, how over the past six months first heavily pregnant and later with the newborn, I had to go everywhere alone, and how I could barely stand the sympathetic looks from the people around me; because we gave to cycling absolutely everything we are and everything we had. I continue about this and that and about some other stuff I can't remember now because of my seething rage. »Now stop whining and piss off and go get that jersey that is rightfully yours!«

Think of me as an angry dictator with horns. Though loving and with a tear in my eye, because I really feel bad for him, however I know that whining won't do any good.

These were literally all psychological tricks I had up my sleeve. And this is just the first day. No way can I survive another Giro.

STAGE TWO

AUGUST 25, 2019
BENIDORM ·······▶ CALPE

200 KM, HILLY

ROGLIČ QUICKLY MADE UP FOR LOST TIME - QUINTANA CLAIMS STAGE TWO

Roche claimed the red jersey. After the crash in the team time trial, Primož Roglič showed his teeth in stage two of the Tour of Spain. He came in third and gained 32 seconds on Miguel Angel Lopez. Nairo Quintana attacked three kilometers before the finish line and claimed the stage victory. The course in the southeast of Spain included **three categorized climbs - two of Category Two and one of the Category Three**. Many were anticipating a sprint in Calpe, but they were wrong.

At the top of the last climb of the day, Puig Llorença, 20 km to the finish line, six favorites surprised the leader Lopez. Nicholas Roche and Mikel Nieve were the first to attack, quickly followed by Quintana, Roglič, Rigoberto Uran, and Fabio Aru. Their lead only increased to the very finish and they managed to gain 37 seconds on the Lopez **group**. The Astana team was not strong enough to catch the **break**. […]

Quintana, who won the Vuelta three years ago and was not at his best in this year's Tour, attacked three kilometers before the finish line and gained five seconds. Roche finished second and Roglič collected four **bonus seconds** for his third place. […] (RTV MMC, 2019b)

IRL	1.	ROCHE, NICOLAS (SUNWEB)	5:26:12
COL	2.	QUINTANA, NAIRO (MOVISTAR)	+2
COL	3.	URAN, RIGOBERTO (EF EDUCATION FIRST)	+8
SLO	6.	ROGLIČ, PRIMOŽ (JUMBO-VISMA)	+36

t's stage two and we're already in the hills. One would think the climbs are classified as difficult and not so difficult, or long and short. But it's not quite like that. In bike races, they're divided into categories, determined by the organizers. Due to subjective views, a precise classification is practically impossible. Some climbs are uncategorized, but that doesn't mean they're not difficult. Sometimes, presumably, the easiest climbs are actually the hardest if the riders choose to make them so with their way of racing.

It makes sense to start with easier ones. Let's take as an example the second stage win in the Tour that Primož achieved in 2018 in the Pyrenees. Usually, the Tour de France rolls into the Alps or the Pyrenees in its second week. Every year it's a different story – there is no rule about that.

So let's take a look at this picture. The easiest category is marked with a 4, a Category 4 climb. These are supposed to be either up to five kilometers long or shorter and steeper. Category Three climbs are more difficult than Category Four: for example, they can be one kilometer long and have a 10% grade or ten kilometers long with a 5% grade.

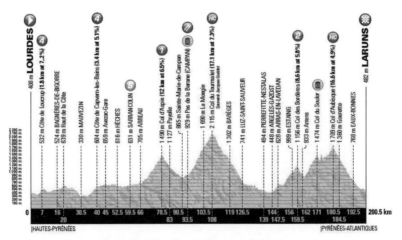

The profile of the Tour de France 2018 stage 19

Category Two continues the trend. The picture shows a Category Two climb that is 8.6 kilometers long and has a grade of 5.8%.

The course profile shows that Col d'Aspin is Category One climb; it's 12 kilometers long and has an average grade of 6.5%.

The highest category is the HC. It marks the climbs that normal people don't want to visit. HC means *hors categorie*, climbs of a special category. We discussed that earlier, with the race classification. The race profile shows the famous Col du Tourmalet with its 17.1 kilometers and a 7.3% average grade. Huh. Scary. Col d'Aubisque is of the same category. The HC category is used only by the French and it won't be found in other races. This category would be marked ESP in Spain. A vertical gain of meters also helps with the categorization of climbs.

Sometimes climbs are categorized differently due to other circumstances and organizers may put a climb of Category One into category HC if it comes at the end of the stage or immediately follows a climb of a similar difficulty. One of the many legends of the Tour offers an insight into the beginnings of categorization. Supposedly they have used the famous Citroën Dyane to categorize the climbs. If that can on four wheels managed to conquer the hill in fourth gear, the climb was categorized as Category Four. Categories Three, Two, and One were established in much the same manner. The glorified HC category Dyane conquered in reverse.

But why do the climbs have to be categorized?

Races are not just about the leader's jersey and stage wins. They also include secondary competitions. And since we're talking about climbs – yes, there is a competition for the best climber. That's the rider who manages to win the most points on the categorized climbs throughout the race. Your answer is correct – the categorization of climbs is necessary to award the points. If you're an amateur cyclist, you know it very well. The riders in the stage races compete for the title of the King of the Mountains. KOM is the most comonly used acronym. In French, it's a little more complicated – they're competing for the Grand Prix de la Montagne or GPM and the best is declared *le meilleur grimpeur*, the best climber. *Voila!*

The rider who collects the most points, available on categorized climbs throughout the stages, has the right to wear the jersey of the leader in the KOM classification. The rider with the highest number of points in the race also wins the KOM title (and jersey) of the race. In the TDF the jersey is called *maillot à pois*, the polka-dot jersey. It's very recognizable, white with red polka dots. The same jersey is also awarded in the Vuelta, only it has a different color scheme, but in the Giro, it's blue, *maglia azzura*. Organizers pick the colors of the category jerseys themselves.

Let's take a look at the Tour de France 2017. The riders climbed 52 categorized climbs during the three weeks. Seven of them were of the HC category, among them, for Slovenians unforgettable, the Col du Galibier, with monstrous 2642 meters of altitude, which brought Slovenia its historic first stage victory in the Tour de France. The first rider to cross the mountain finish was Primož Roglič, who took 20 KOM points. The second

THE CIRCLE OF DEATH

IN 1910, THE TOUR DE FRANCE MADE ITS WAY OVER HIGH MOUNTAINS FOR THE FIRST TIME. AND WHAT MOUNTAINS! STAGE TEN WAS 312 KILOMETERS LONG AND CLIMBED OVER FIVE ICONIC PYRENEAN PASSES – THE COL DE PEYRESOURDE, COL D'ASPIN, COL DU TOURMALET, COL DU SOULOR, AND THE COL D'AUBISQUE.

THE TOUR DIRECTOR HENRI DESGRANGE WAS AMPING UP THE TENSION IN THE PRESS FOR MONTHS BEFORE THE STAGE. SOME RIDERS DIDN'T WANT TO START BECAUSE ORGANIZERS DIDN'T PROVIDE PROTECTION FROM BEARS. NO ONE REALLY KNEW WHAT TO EXPECT WHEN THEY MADE THEIR WAY INTO THE WILD MOUNTAINS. ON JULY 21 AT 3.30 AM, THE HEROES TOOK OFF FROM BAGNÈRES-DE-LUCHON. ONLY ONE RIDER MADE IT TO THE TOP OF TOURMALET WITHOUT GETTING OFF HIS BIKE. THE ROADS WERE HARSH DIRT PATHS, COVERED IN ROCKS.

THE ORGANIZERS WERE ANXIOUSLY WAITING AT THE TOP OF THE LAST PASS, THE AUBISQUE, TO SEE WHETHER ANY OF THE RIDERS WOULD MAKE IT UP THERE.

FINALLY, SOMEONE MADE IT! AN UNKNOWN FRANÇOIS LAFOURCADE RODE BY QUIETLY WITH HIS HEAD DOWN. FIFTEEN MINUTES LATER, ANOTHER RIDER SHOWED UP, OCTAVE LAPIZE, OTHERWISE AN EXCELLENT CLIMBER. THIS TIME, HE WAS WALKING, PUSHING THE BIKE AND LOUDLY CURSING, LIVID. WHEN HE FINALLY REACHED THE TOP, HE SHOUTED AT THE ORGANIZERS: »VOUS ÊTES DES ASSASSINS! OUI, DES ASSASSINS!« YOU'RE MURDERERS! YES, MURDERERS! THERE WERE 160 KILOMETERS TO GO, AND EVEN THOUGH LAPIZE THREATENED TO ABANDON AFTER THE DESCENT, HE WON THE STAGE AND LATER ALSO THE RACE.

WITH THE DANGEROUS PYRENEES AND THE SHOUTING ABOUT ASSASSINS, THE LEGEND WAS BORN. DESGRANGE'S NEWSPAPER L'AUTO NAMED THE ROUTE FROM PEYRESOURDE TO AUBISQUE THE CIRCLE OF DEATH. »WHERE DREAMS OF IMMORTALITY GO TO DIE. WHERE MEN ARE COMPLETELY BROKEN EMOTIONALLY, PHYSICALLY, PSYCHOLOGICALLY, AND SPIRITUALLY.« (VELOPELOTON 2014).

rider took 15, the third 12 points, and so on all the way to the eighth rider, who took 2. There were eleven Category One climbs, with 10 points for the first rider, 8 for the second, 6 for the third, and so on to 1 point for the sixth. Points are awarded on every categorized climb, but that's probably of no interest to you – unless you want to fight for the polka-dot jersey.

The greater the difficulty of the climb, the more riders are awarded the points. If the stage finishes on top of a categorized climb, the points are doubled.

Understanding the points system, we can see that the KOM is not necessarily the rider who is the best climber, but rather the rider who collects the points most consistently. He probably started the race with this objective in mind, as it requires a bit of planning. The roadbook contains a clear information of how many points are available in each stage and where exactly they are, so the riders can calculate in which stages the breakaway might pay off if they're interested in the polka-dot jersey. One has to choose smartly.

Oh, a breakaway?

Let's say you're watching a race on TV from the very start. A few riders are franticly jumping ahead and trying to gain as much of a lead in front of the peloton as they can. Riders who want to make a successful breakaway start attacking almost immediately after the start.

Why would anyone want to be battered by the wind, when they could more comfortably ride within the group? Mostly for these reasons:

> the breakaway is joined by riders who want to win the stage, but don't feel like brawling with the whole peloton at the finish line

> breaking away is certain team's tactic

> riders in the breakaway will show off the sponsor logos on their jersey in live TV coverage, and the sponsors will be ecstatic

> any number of other reasons I can't think of right now

And the peloton?

In bike racing, the peloton is the main group with the majority of the riders. You've probably also heard expressions like the pack or the bunch. The leader's jersey is somewhere in the peloton most of the time.

When riders race tightly together, they conserve energy because they're drafting – which is of course not the case for those in the frontline, cutting the wind drag. The camera sometimes shows the back of the peloton, too, which the French call *arrière du peloton* – the rear of the peloton.

You're probably a bit confused now. When the peloton breaks apart during difficult climbs and some riders are left riding alone, it's not a breakaway and you can't tell if the peloton even exists anymore – usually, just a small group remains with the rider in the leader's jersey. In time, you'll of course get a grip on recognizing the different formations. But let's get back to our breakaway.

It usually takes some time before the breakaway settles and forms completely. The first attempt is rarely successful. The riders keep attacking; some want to join in and help them, while the teams are carefully monitoring the dynamics and thwarting attacks they don't like.

An attack will only be successful if it suits the strongest teams or those who have certain ambitions. For example – if a rider, who is a threat to a certain team leader in the general classification, wants to make a break, that leader's team will neutralize the attack and won't allow it to break away. It's much the same with neutralizing attacks that are not to the liking of teams that want to give their sprinters a chance at the end of the stage. The riders communicate with each other personally or by radio transmitters. When the breakaway settles, usually in the first two hours of the race, the Radio Tour[26], which regularly updates all the team

---

[26] Radio Tour is not an entertaining radio station playing top hits for the riders. The communication during the race is a very interesting thing.

cars about what is happening[27] on the road, communicates who's in the breakaway, while sports directors pass that information to their riders via another radio frequency. The riders in the breakaway are accompanied by a motorcycle, carrying a board showing their time advantage over the peloton.

Everything is happening very quickly and in a very stressful environment, so the riders constantly have to be ready for quick reactions, but above all, they always have to be alert. Sometimes the breakaway doesn't form for quite a while, making the beginning of the race even harder and more stressful than the end.

If somehow a large group manages to ride away, we can say we have two pelotons on the road. The most common expression for a breakaway, at least to me, is the Italian word *fuga*. Sometimes we also hear the word escape, in French *échappée*. The Spanish word for the riders in the breakaway is *escapados*. One of the terms is also *cabeza de carrera* or *tête de la course*, the head of the race.

When the breakaway takes the form and size that the peloton is happy with, the main group slows down considerably. If you pay attention, it will seem as if they're not racing, but having a relaxed Sunday ride. Sometimes the camera catches the whole group stopping and taking a leak.

The leisurely ride doesn't last long – the teams must control the race and not let the breakaway gain too much of an advantage. If the time gap narrows, some riders who wanted to join the first breakaway but missed it may feel the urge to try again by attacking from the peloton. That means more work for the teams who have to control the race.

They control it by dictating the tempo at the front of the peloton. If they let the breakaway to get too far ahead, they can have another problem – how to catch it.

---

[27] Including crashes, time differences, mechanical failures, attacks etc.

A breakaway attempt

But, as life is not just black and white, this, of course, is not the only scenario. Sometimes the peloton may choose not to chase the breakaway and sometimes the race leader's team might decide they're not the only ones who should take responsibility for controlling the race, so they let someone else pick up the slack – as they look at each other and try to shift responsibility, the breakaway only increases its advantage.

Teams might use the same tactics when they don't want their closest rivals to win the bonus seconds awarded at the finish line – they don't chase the breakaway and thus the bonus seconds are not available for the others in the peloton, presuming, of course, the escape is made by at least three riders. We probably won't see the team leaders in the breakaway.

I have digressed slightly from the main topic, but the breakaways add an interesting dynamic in cycling, and figuring out whether they'll survive or not and working out the tactics of those riders sent to the front line is much too entertaining.

To continue where I was before the swerving off the path – chasing breakaways generally begins in the second half of the stage. The rule of thumb says that the peloton, working in unison, gains about one minute every ten kilometers on the breakaway. But that's just in theory and a lot depends on the terrain, the weather – above all the wind – the quality of the riders in the breakaway, their collaboration and, of course, the desire of the group behind them to chase it (or not). For the escape to be successful at the beginning, the riders must work together – every single one of them has to contribute their part at the front of the breakaway, much like in the team time trial, with the difference being that riders of different teams are racing together.

The unwritten rule states that the work at the front of the bunch must be done by the race leader's team. As I mentioned before, the teams that think a successful breakaway might somehow harm them should help, too – the breakaway might spoil their plans for the end of the stage or for the general classification.

And when does a breakaway finally crumble? It's hard to say, but – the closer to the finish line, the better. If the escapees are caught too quickly, there's a chance of new attacks and new breakaways.

As long as the breakaway is in front, the race is under control. When it's neutralized, the attacks begin all over again (and that's exactly what happened in the stage two of the Vuelta). In theory, teams that don't want new attacks after the breakaway is caught should dictate a fast pace at the front of the peloton to prevent new attempts.

Sometimes the breakaway is caught literally a few meters before the finish line. And sometimes the winner comes from the breakaway. Some stages in Grand Tours are designed to be breakaway days in advance.

But that's only on paper; there are 176 riders at the start and there's a lot of external factors that they can't influence. Winning from a breakaway is a great way for a rider from a smaller team to win a stage in a three-week race.

It's important to mention one thing. Well, two; in most cases, the breakaway succeeds if the peloton decides to let it succeed. The other thing is that the way cyclists ride in stage races differs from how they ride during one-day races. Successful escapes are very rare in one-day races – but a word of caution, we're talking about the first breakaways that come right after the start of the race. It often happens that the winner of the race comes from the second, the third, or the umpteenth breakaway, carried out as a fierce attack or an acceleration that only a few other riders manage to follow.

Whether the breakaway is caught or not depends on the strength and line-up of the teams in the peloton, and of course on their interests. I think we already mentioned somewhere that teams with a rider in the breakaway won't chase it. In a way, it's not necessary, therefore we rarely see riders from the same team working in the front of a breakaway and in the peloton.

There's a number of meetings on the team busses before the start of every stage. Sending your rider into the breakaway is also a part of your tactics. When a stage finishes with a climb, it's good if the team leader has his last domestique in the breakaway. Typically, in stages with summit finishes the breakaway is caught very late. As the bunch falls apart, and only a handful of very strong riders remain - sometimes only the team leaders and the best climbers - it's good if you have one of your teammates still higher up the road. Should the leader have a mechanical or a crash, the domestique would drop back to give him his bike, while he would wait for the team car or the neutral race support.

Speaking of vehicles – if the breakaway has more than one-minute advantage on the peloton, the race commissar allows the team cars of teams with riders in the breakaway to overtake the bunch. This way they're in the right place in the event of a mechanical or a crash, and the riders in front have food and drink available.

There's also a neutral service vehicle available to all the riders and they can use it when their team car is too far behind and there's no teammate in sight to help. The neutral vehicle carries spare bikes, wheels, and a mechanic. But this is only a temporary solution; every rider will, if and when he has a chance, call his team car and exchange the neutral bike for his own spare bike, set up specifically for him.

> **❝** *The neutral vehicle is just … there. In my experience, it's not used very often. Firstly, the equipment might not suit you, that is, if the race is sponsored by a certain provider, it's entirely possible you won't be able to use the bike because your team uses something completely different and you won't even be able to clip into the pedals. Something like that happened to Chris Froome at Mont Ventoux[28] – the bike didn't suit him.*
>
> *Secondly, if the neutral vehicle comes, at some point your team car will show up, too. If you need it, you call it over the radio. OK, if this doesn't happen at a decisive moment in the race, you have time to drop to the back of the peloton and raise your hand. The commissar, who is in the first vehicle in the convoy, will radio all the teams a mes- sage, let's say, number 176, Team Jumbo-Visma, assistance; saying that, he'll give the team car permission to drive ahead and slowly work its way through the riders etc. The car always needs permission to overtake the convoy. And sometimes it just can't reach you. In that case, you wait by the side of the road, all miserable, and hope some- one will remember you as soon as possible, or that a rider from your team will come along, hopefully not seven feet tall.* **❞**

The biggest time difference between a breakaway and the peloton? The German Jens Voigt won stage 13 of Tour de France in 2006 with a solo attack from a breakaway. The remaining five riders who were in the breakaway with him crossed the finish line lagging between 40 seconds to more than 6 minutes behind, while the bunch came in 29 minutes and 57 seconds behind the winner.

But there's enough material to write a series of books about breakaways, the rationale behind them, incidents, anecdotes, and possible scenarios, so at this point, I'll just let the breakaway go its merry way, wherever it wants to go.

The riders finishing in the front will always get the most attention.

Anyway, the first three places in a stage carry bonus seconds. Quintana got a 10-second bonus as the winner, Roche, who came in second, got 6 seconds, and Roglič, who finished third, got 4. Those four seconds will be deducted from Primož's overall time – the riders fighting for the best position in the GC want to have as low overall time as possible.

The GC standings changed considerably; the six riders gained a lot with their successful attack in the last 20 kilometers, among them Roglič who moved up to 6th place in the GC fight (from 99th).

---

[28] Many fans might remember stage 12 of the Tour in 2016. A huge crowd on the last climb stopped the camera motorbike and three riders crashed into it, among them Froome in the yellow jersey. Even though he called for assistance, the team car couldn't drive up to him. The neutral vehicle provided a replacement bike, but he couldn't use it. So he carried on on foot – actually he ran until he got his own bike. There was a lot of debate after the stage, but his team and the race management agreed to erase the time that Froome had lost due to the special circumstances.

THE COMEBACK

Sunday, August 25, 2019

Idly, not burdening myself too much, I'm trying to figure out what can happen on the first Vuelta Sunday. There was a fucking earthquake yesterday. A shock. Maybe the Vuelta was decided yesterday and some residual anger, mixed in a cocktail with some adrenaline and sadness, is still clinging on to me. And it hurts. No one is watching television because today's stage is supposed to be one of those where commentators have to fill the dead air with blabbering about the beaches, olive oil, and citrus orchards. In TDF, they'd probably go on and on about châteaux, moldy cheeses, and vineyards. The knucklehead on a bike vehemently stated before the start that " nothing's gonna happen today, especially not for the GC ". With the baby handed over to grandparents, Vinko and I are sprawled between the hall and the living room, partially watching the race and partially doing something more entertaining.

The breakaway is pulled back much too early. Pelotón agrupado, write the Spanish. Italians would call it gruppo compatto. We just say they are all back together. The peloton cracks while pedaling up a steep climb and what is supposed to be a compact train of riders is more like a colorful scruffy bunch of willful sheep not listening to their shepherd. They've blown to pieces.

The grade must be neck-breaking, considering they're all electrified and are reacting to the slightest move of a bike to their side, in front or behind them. They're churning over that knoll that offers a view of the sandy beaches of Alicante. The town with dull apartment buildings is stifled under the heat, which is radiating from the ground. He, his team, the whole protour came here to prepare. The main thing is he doesn't fall too far behind if he gets dropped somehow. He'd say this climb is one of the 'fuck you climbs', short and brutally steep ascents.

Hop, hop, jump after jump, a black and yellow jersey is there. And it's one of ours!!! Not just ours, it's my Primi.

And then it quickly becomes clear the attack is too strong to let it go. A small group of team leaders, it will surely bother someone who's fallen behind. It won't happen.

I'm running up and down trying to convince myself to be indifferent. Ten kilometers pass and the situation on the road is the same. They should have been caught by now? What the hell is going on? It turns out the red jersey lost his herd on the last climb and there was no one to do the critical job at the head of the bunch. Fine by me, even though I don't believe it quite yet. Maybe the time graphic is broken.

They're stomping ahead and there's not a force in the world that could stop them. They won't catch them. I'm tiptoeing around obsessively, glimpsing through the window and trying to find someone to share the joy with.

It's all about the stage win now and who will gain in the GC. He could win this; he's the best sprinter in this group. Expectations, expectations, going from hoping that we won't go home to wanting the whole world and more in just 24 hours.

Something's not right if Quintana dropped him on the flat and the Columbian is not caught before the finish line, but that doesn't matter. Yesterday's lacerations are an insignificant inconvenience compared to today's performance. The race falls into place by itself. If you're worthy of it, it lets you get back into the game.

The resurrection of the yellow phoenix, who's stubbornly making his way to the top as if trudging through fresh snow somewhere among the peaks, where my being resides in some distant dreams, flattening the peaks, plummeting into the valleys like an eagle and co-creating, no, not co-creating, pushing himself into the endlessness. And it was only the second stage of the race. I admire his mental toughness.

A phoenix whose wings burned yellow, so he could fly again. Even though he couldn't sprint for the win because he almost fell off the bike due to cramps. Did my phone lecture yesterday help? I don't know and I couldn't care less as long as we're back in the game.

STAGE THREE

MEZGEC THIRD AT THE VUELTA: »I COULD ONLY FIGHT FOR CRUMBS«

Roglič won a bonus second in the intermediate sprint. Luka Mezgec came in third in stage three of the Tour of Spain, the field sprint was convincingly taken by Sam Bennett. [...]

Nicholas Roche kept the lead in the general classification. Primož Roglič remains in 6th. He was third across the intermediate sprint, after 167 kilometers, and won one bonus second. Angel Madrazo, Oscar Cebado, and Hector Saez rode away from the bunch immediately after the start in the town of Ibi. The breakaway managed to gain over five-minute advantage, but, 40 kilometers shy of the finish line, the peloton (where Roglič's team Jumbo-Visma were very active) chased it down. The Tuesday stage will also be to the liking of sprinters, and on Wednesday the favorites will finally start the fight for the general classification in a difficult stage with the finish in Javalambre. [...] (RTV MMC 2019c)

IRL	1. ROCHE, NICOLAS (SUNWEB)	9:51:14	
COL	2. QUINTANA, NAIRO (MOVISTAR)	+2	
COL	3. URAN, RIGOBERTO (EF EDUCATION FIRST)	+8	
SLO	6. ROGLIČ, PRIMOŽ (JUMBO-VISMA)	+35	

If the climbs are where the light riders, the climbers, fight it out, the sprint is quite the opposite of that.

The sprinters don't do well in mountains and much the same, although not necessarily, the climbers aren't well versed in scrunching into ideal sprinting position at 80 km/h. Sprinting is kind of a chaos that starts to brew at least 20 kilometers before the finish line. It can start even earlier if the terrain is demanding and dangerous, for example, if there are a lot of roundabouts, narrowings, and so on. Every sprinter has his train – teammates, who in the final kilometers form a sprint train, trying to get their sprinter into the ideal position for the sprint finish.

The sprinter is last in the lead-out, conserving energy by drafting, while his lead-out men »peel off« one by one as their work is done.

But that is an ideal scenario. In reality, sprinters often hustle and push each other; sometimes there isn't enough space for all, the lead-out falls apart and they lose their last man. Due to the very high speed, there could also be crashes.

The last kilometer is a special area and riders practically don't use the breaks. It is usually visibly marked with an inflatable arch under which the riders zoom through. There's a recognizable red triangular flag hanging from it in the middle that French call *la flamme rouge*. In Italian, it's called *ultimo chilometro*, but Slovenians found an interesting name for it – because of its red color and longish form, hanging over the road, we call it the devil's tongue.

If you ever watch a sprint live, I can assure you that you'll see pretty much nothing. It will probably be best for you to pull your head behind the railing like a turtle, because you have a fair chance you'll get an unintentional whack on your nose. Also, put away your smartphone, especially if you're standing in the first row. It's much like if you're standing in a swamp, full of hungry alligators with a juicy steak in your hand. In the end, the winner is the rider who is the most resourceful in the chaos, who is the best at

La flamme rouge and two Slovenians on bikes

pushing his way through, who is the strongest, who conserves enough energy, and who follows the right wheel in front of him – until, in the decisive moment, he slings past and crosses the finish line. Above all, it's the rider who stays on his bike. Good timing is very important, too. But that's just my opinion, as I have no clue about sprinting.

PANIER DE CRABES

THE FRENCH ARE PARTICULAR, AND THEY CHOOSE EXPRESSIONS ACCORDINGLY. THE MOMENT THE TEAMS START TO PREPARE AND GROUP INTO A FORMATION OF A SPRINT TRAIN, RIDERS PUSH AND MOVE IN EVERY DIRECTION. THE FRENCH CALL THAT A BASKET FULL OF CRABS.

Much like the climbers fight for the climber's jersey in the mountains, the sprinters are fighting for their own – in the Giro, it's *maglia ciclamino* which is kind of a mauve color. In the Tour it's green.

The green jersey in the TDF is awarded to the best sprinter and the points are collected in the intermediate sprints and sprint finishes. The intermediate sprint is a point in the stage that is marked in the profile in advance. A certain number of riders can collect points counting towards the green jersey.

If you ever look at the profile of an Italian race, don't expect to see a television set where it says TV. Italians call the intermediate sprint *traguardo volante*, or simply TV.

Maillot vert, as the jersey is named in the TDF, will be won by the best sprinter. Points are awarded for every stage, but most points can be collected in flat stages and intermediate sprints[29]. In a flat stage, for example, where we expect to get the winner with the sprint finish, he will win 50 points in the green jersey competition.

Let's say the Slovak Peter Sagan won. The next stage will be a difficult one with the finish at the top of the mountain pass. Let's say that one is won by one of the Columbians, who are renowned

---

[29] Every race has its own rules about where and when the points are awarded.

climbers. The Columbian will collect 20 green points[30] for his win. As many as Sagan would win if he'd be first in the intermediate sprint.

In the Tour of Spain, this story is green but completely different. The Vuelta's green jersey is won by the best rider in the points classification. The Spaniards award the same number of points in all of the stages down to 15th place, but very few in the bonus sprints.

Primož Roglič won 25 points for his ITT win, as many as Sam Bennett for his win in a flat stage and Tadej Pogačar for his win in a mountain stage. So what have we learned? Sagan wouldn't like the Vuelta very much. All kidding aside, we learned that the same colors don't have the same meaning in different races. Green isn't always green.

So it's clear why Primož Roglič, and not the best sprinter, won the green jersey in the 2019 Vuelta: he won one stage, he came second and third three times, etc.

---

[30] And quite a lot of points for the climber's jersey.

STAGE FOUR

AUGUST 27, 2019

CULLERA ·······▶ EL PUIG

176 KM, FLAT

YOUNG JAKOBSEN WINS, MEZGEC FORUTH;
ROGLIČ'S TEAMMATE KRUIJSWIJK ABANDONS THE RACE

[…] The Dutch champion Fabio Jakobsen was the fastest in the sprint finish in
stage four of the Tour of Spain. Luka Mezgec was in the mix for the highest
places again, but he finished just behind the best, in fourth place. […] The
start of stage four was more to the north, in Cullera. On the 175.5-kilometer
route the cyclists first circled Valencia before returning to the coast, and
finishing in El Puig. The riders had to climb a short, Category Three slope
about 45 kilometers before the finish line, but the climb didn't significantly
help in whittling down the bunch. The last 20 kilometers after the descent were
completely flat, which gave the peloton a chance to chase down the breakaway.
This meant the sprinting elite could battle it out for the second day in a row,
this time in El Puig.

There were no changes at the top of the general classification, so Roglič
remained in sixth place. […] The wind was quite strong in the last part of the
stage, causing the peloton to split in two. The favorites were careful enough,
so they all finished in the first group, including Roglič and Tadej Pogačar.
Irishman Nicolas Roche kept the red jersey. […] (RTV MMC 2019č)

IRL	1.	ROCHE, NICOLAS (SUNWEB)	13:55:30
COL	2.	QUINTANA, NAIRO (MOVISTAR)	+2
COL	3.	URAN, RIGOBERTO (EF EDUCATION FIRST)	+8
SLO	6.	ROGLIČ, PRIMOŽ (JUMBO-VISMA)	+35

Nothing happened that you wouldn't already know. Roglič's team-mate Kruijswijk abandoned the race because he was still feeling the consequences of the crash in stage one. That means his result would be marked as DNF[31], did not finish. In Spanish they call it *abandon*. When a rider abandons, another rider cannot replace him. To put it plainly, there is no reserve bench in the cycling races. So Primož had only six teammates left. If a rider doesn't finish a stage, it means he's finished with the race.

But in Spain, there were more people than just the seven riders of Jumbo-Visma left. If you think the riders are the only people at the races, you're dead wrong. Teams are enormous; they're more like small traveling companies, and the work they do might not be done on the road, but it's just as crucial for the whole machine to work properly.

❝ *There's a huge number of people with us, especially at the biggest races. Sometimes I don't know that someone is one of us, and then I see he's wearing our gear. Us, riders are mostly in contact with sports directors, soigneurs and mechanics. We speak to the DS every day before, during, and after the stage: we're trying to carry out their orders on the road as much as possible. We spend a lot of time with soigneurs; during the massage, they hand us food during the race, wait for us at the finish and take us where the protocol requires us to be. If you're not the stage winner or you don't have one of the jerseys, they tell you where the team bus is parked and where the hotel is.*

There's a big crowd behind the finish line, and it can be dangerous – photographers, cameramen, reporters who are waiting for a statement, organizers, officials, special guests. At the big races, sometimes there can be couple of tasks the organizer requires you for, however you always get a chance to quickly freshen up first.

---

[31] A similar abbreviation is DNS, meaning did not start.

Soigneur's help is so handy in such moments. The organizer has a different man for every task; one takes you from the tent to the podium; there is another one on the podium, telling you what to do; and the third one that takes you to the anti-doping control, etc. The whole race organization is unbelievable, and there's a lot of people involved. You have to have a master's degree to find your way in such an enormous system. The organizer takes care of all the hotels we sleep in during the race, and the logistics are at a really high level.

As far as the team is concerned, we have a whole squad of mechanics, a bus driver, cooks, medical team, i.e., a doctor and an osteopath, public relations representatives, some take care of re-porters, some of social media, and some of sponsors.

A sponsor's representative joins us sometimes, so they can experience the race live, from the team car, for instance. The general manager and photographers are also present, of course, a cameraman and a director of sorts, and sometimes there's a nutritionist, too. We have someone who organizes our travels to and from the race; getting 30 people from 30 places, scattered all over the world, to one point is not an easy feat. And the riders, after all - we had riders from the Netherlands, the USA, Germany, New Zealand, and Slovenia in the Vuelta team - come from different corners of the planet.

We have guys on Grand Tours who carry our mattresses. It sounds funny, but it makes sense. Twenty-one stages, two rest days, a day after and three days before the race, make almost a month, and we change hotel every day, except at the beginning and maybe on a rest day when we stay put. Sleeping on the same mattresses helps the riders regenerate as much as possible. This makes more work for the team, of course. Every morning after breakfast, they pack up our mattresses, load them into a truck, and drive them straight to the next hotel. They dismantle eight beds and put them back together there, so they're ready for us when we arrive at the new hotel after the stage.

The hotels, too, must meet some special requirements – we never make reservations ourselves. Our staff does that, and we just receive room numbers on our phones. Many times our cooks cook our meals in hotel kitchens. Water must be available outside the hotel so our mechanics can wash the bikes, cars, and busses, etc. They have to be immaculate all the time because of the sponsors. Our convoy uses a whole lot of electricity, but most of all, water. The bus has showers we use after every stage, so the tank has to be filled up. On our truck, which is modified, of course, we have refrigerators, cupboards with food, and two washing machines that are running all the time. We wash our rags every day; each rider has a washing bag with his name on and soigneurs take the dirty laundry away and bring it back clean.

There's also a food room in every hotel – a room where we have food available, a lot of food. Snacks and drinks for when we get hunger attacks between the meals. There is no lunch during the races. Oh, well, there is, if you will, but we eat while racing, and the dinners are very late.

We also have staff who disinfects door handles, rooms, etc. We come into contact with a lot of people during the big races, and we have to limit the chance of infections as much as possible. **”**

I'm not a big fan of numbers, but these are extraordinary. There will always be up to 176 riders at the start of the Grand Tour. Every team will have 20 to 30 staff members.

The Tour de France is seen by about 12 million people every year – 12 million! They are standing by the side of the road, waiting for skinny guys in soaking wet Spandex with chafed asses for seven hours a day on average.

There are 35,000 people responsible for safety, who make sure they don't jump all over the road or do some other stupid thing. Crazy, isn't it?

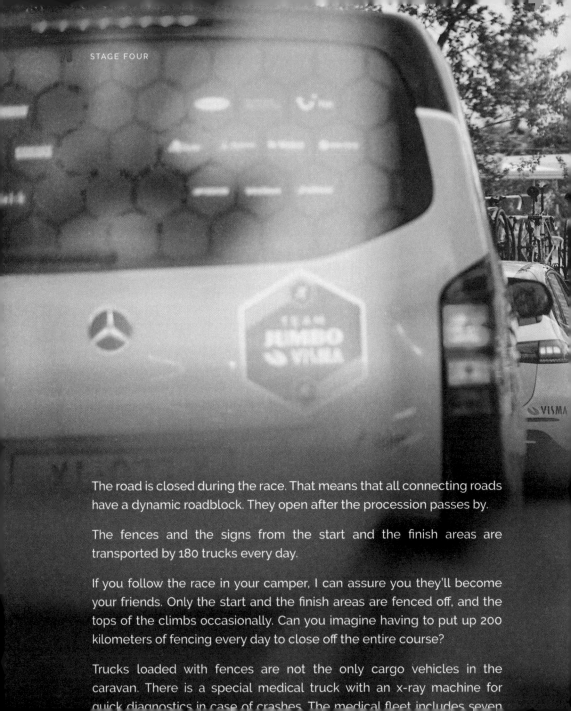

The road is closed during the race. That means that all connecting roads have a dynamic roadblock. They open after the procession passes by.

The fences and the signs from the start and the finish areas are transported by 180 trucks every day.

If you follow the race in your camper, I can assure you they'll become your friends. Only the start and the finish areas are fenced off, and the tops of the climbs occasionally. Can you imagine having to put up 200 kilometers of fencing every day to close off the entire course?

Trucks loaded with fences are not the only cargo vehicles in the caravan. There is a special medical truck with an x-ray machine for quick diagnostics in case of crashes. The medical fleet includes seven

ambulances, two medical cars, a motorbike, ten doctors, and ten nurses. Of course, we all hope they have as little work as possible.

The new technology means that nowadays almost everybody can watch races. Daam Van Reeth states in his newspaper article, Forecasting Tour de France TV Audiences, there are on average 25 million people watching each stage on TV.

But the way the picture makes it to the small screen is a really complicated procedure. Camera motorbikes (and an audio motorbike) and helicopters with a camera, flying low above the riders, send the signal to the helicopters flying higher, at 800 meters – these are merely the transmitters. These then send the signal to airplanes, which relay it to

STAGE FIVE

AUGUST 28, 2019

L'ELIANA ┈┈┈▶ OBSERVATORIO ASTROFÍSICO DE JAVALAMBRE

171 KM, MOUNTAIN

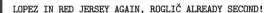

LOPEZ IN RED JERSEY AGAIN, ROGLIČ ALREADY SECOND!

Pogačar is already among the ten best riders in the general classification. The first mountain stage of this year's Tour of Spain brought a new leading rider in the general classification. That is Miguel Angel Lopez. Angel Madrazo won the stage. Primož Roglič came in 6th, Tadej Pogačar 7th! […]

The Astana team leader attacked about two kilometers from the finish line and managed to attain the decisive advantage, finishing 12 seconds in front of 6th-placed Primož Roglič (Jumbo-Visma), who climbed from 6th to 2nd in the general classification (+0:14)!

ROCHE HIT THE WALL, LOPEZ GOT THE RED JERSEY

The fight for the general classification was especially exciting. On the final climb, the peloton, consisting of about 50 riders, fell apart; quite a few riders hit the wall, among them Roche, who was leading the race, Uran and Majka. Lopez attacked about 2.2 kilometers before the finish line, Alejandro Valverde and both Slovenes, Roglič and Pogačar, followed. The first to cross the finish line was Madrazo, who attacked with 200 meters to go and finished in 4 hours, 58 minutes, and 31 seconds. […] (RTV MMC 2019d)

COL 1. LOPEZ MORENO, MIGUEL ANGEL (ASTANA PRO)   18:55:21

SLO 2. ROGLIČ, PRIMOŽ (JUMBO-VISMA)   +14

COL 3. QUINTANA, NAIRO (MOVISTAR)   +23

A successful breakaway that managed to hold on. Don't worry; no one hit the wall. That is just an expression used when a rider runs out of glycogen reserves in his muscles, out of energy, and loses all his power – when he almost stops. Roche lost all the energy in this stage and, with it, the red jersey.

And Alejandro? What about him? If you ever watched a race, you've surely seen him. Maybe you even asked yourself why the hell does one guy have a completely different jersey than others. The rainbow jersey – and a gold medal, of course – belongs to the current world champion, and Alejandro Valverde won the WC in 2018. We can easily distinguish him in the peloton from all others by it. Any winner of the world champion title has the right to wear a rainbow on their collar and sleeves[32] to the end of his career.

The UCI World Championship is held every year at the end of September. So what now? Does Primož ride for Jumbo-Visma or Slovenia?

National team riders are employed by various teams from all over the world. In the World Championship, they wear the national jersey with their own team sponsors, so every national jersey is different. They also ride with equipment provided by their teams. But they ride for Slovenia.

Let's say Matej Mohorič, Luka Mezgec, and Primož Roglič (along with others) represent Slovenia in a road race. These three cyclists ride for three different teams. They all have Slovenia written on their backs, but on the shorts and specific spots, as strictly designated by the rules, they wear team sponsors. They also ride their own team bikes, with their team shoes, helmets, glasses, and other equipment.

The World Championship races are unique in many ways. The number of riders in national teams is determined by points that riders of the same nationality collect through the season[33]. The WC is not included in the

---

[32] The same goes for the national champions and their national flag colors.
[33] Four to eight riders.

UCI WorldTour and the road race must be 250 to 280 kilometers long. The World (and many times the national) Championship route consists of laps,[34] so to attract many spectators.

The elite category includes an individual time trial. Now there's also a new discipline, the mixed relay, with teams consisting of two women and two men.

—

[34] If a rider is lapped by the leaders, he's eliminated from the race.

The rainbow and the red jersey

STAGE SIX

AUGUST 29, 2019

MORA DE RUBIELOS ·······▶ ARES DEL MAESTRAT

199 KM, HILLY

POGAČAR ATTACKED IN THE GROUP OF FAVORITES, URAN AND ROCHE ABANDONED [...]

Stage six of the Tour of Spain, marked by a massive crash in the peloton and Nicolas Roche and Rigoberto Uran abandoning, was won by the local Jesus Herrada after a successful breakaway. Dylan Teuns took the red jersey. [...]

When the riders in the breakaway crossed the finish line, the peloton with the GC's favorites had one and a half kilometers to go. That's when Tadej Pogačar, riding in the white jersey of the best young rider, attacked. [...] He crossed the finish line as 11th. Primož Roglič came in 16th, right behind Lopez, Nairo Quintana, and Alejandro Valverde (both Movistar). [...]

Somewhere in the middle of the stage, the peloton was split in two by a **massive crash**. [...] Irishman Roche (Sunweb), who was leading the GC until Wednesday, sought **medical help** and had to abandon the race a few minutes later. Jumbo-Visma's Tony Martin, George Bennett, and Neilson Powless also crashed.

Roglič is now 4th, Pogačar 10th. [...] The 199-kilometer stage from Mora de Rubielos to Ares del Maestrat has been designed for breakaways. [...] The GC favorites were, as expected, paying attention to each other. [...] (RTV MMC 2019e)

BEL	1.	TEUNS, DYLAN (BAHRAIN-MERIDA)	23:44:00	
ESP	2.	DE LA CRUZ MELGAREJO, DAVID (INEOS)	+38	
COL	3.	LOPEZ MORENO, MIGUEL ANGEL (ASTANA PRO)	+1:00	
SLO	4.	ROGLIČ, PRIMOŽ (JUMBO-VISMA)	+1:14	

Ah, the crashes. We don't like to see them, we don't want to hear about them, and the riders equally don't want to hit the ground. But, like it or not, crashes are a part of what they do much more than in most other sports. The sooner you accept this fact, the better – even though you never accept it completely.

Why do crashes occur? There are at least as many reasons as there are riders. They're quite common in sprints because sprinters are audacious and, speaking plainly, a bit nuts (and I'm not in any way suggesting other riders are entirely sane). If you ever have a chance to watch a helicopter recording of a finish sprint (from a bird's-eye view), you'll see that they're not just good riders but also excellent brawlers. They're pushing their way to where there's no room, shoving each other into the fences, butting their helmets and knocking their elbows, leaning into one another ... They're a temperamental and explosive bunch – like their muscles. Usually, they all make it over the finish line on two wheels. Sometimes some have to hit the brakes, they lose the speed and their position, and with those the chance of better result; in the worst case, they crash.

Of course, crashes are not only a part of sprints. In the peloton, they can be caused merely by two wheels touching, someone losing their balance, someone looking back, a momentary lapse in attention, a wet road, a roundabout, etc.

You can crash all by yourself, or someone can knock you over. You can ride off the road, or you can hit a stop sign. A dog that slipped off the leash may cross your way, or you can ride over a flag that a kid sticks out onto a road a bit too much. There are increasing instances of crashes caused by camera motorbikes, other vehicles in the race, and fans looking at their phones instead of the road.

Do you remember how Vincenzo Nibali and Primož crashed in the Tour of 2018 in the Alpe d'Huez stage? The culprit was a fan's photo camera band hanging over the fence that Nibali caught with his handlebars.

There are thousands of reasons. The first time I was at the team training camp in the Sierra Nevada, I found it hilarious how all those seasoned cyclists feared the roundabouts around Granada. Andalusia is otherwise known for olive oil. During the olive picking season, trailers haul heaps of this highly bouncy, tiny fruit, which tends to jump out onto the road. The asphalt stays greasy the whole year.

The safest position to avoid crashes is the head of the peloton. You see everything that's happening on the road, and everything in your way; there are fewer riders in front of you, if any at all. But getting to the front and staying there is a difficult task. And even there, you're not entirely safe.

If you're somewhere in the middle of the bunch and a crash happens, you can stay behind even if you didn't fall. In massive crashes, the peloton splits, and before the poor souls pick themselves up from underneath their bikes – we're delighted if all of them get up – those who avoided the crash keep riding.

What happens when a rider falls? If he's not hurt too much, he gets back on his bike and keeps riding. But, first, he checks whether his bike is ridable. Teammates can help him with their equipment and give him a tow so he can catch the peloton (we know already that wind is the worst enemy). The rider can also call the team car to get a new wheel or bike. Everything happens under the assumption that the crash was not too hard, and it's possible to act swiftly.

Even though the vehicles' place in the caravan is constantly changing, there is a specific order that should be maintained. Before the first stage, teams draw stickers, kind of like starting numbers for the cars that decide position of each car in the row. For instance, at the Tour de France 2018 that began with a regular stage, the Jumbo-Visma Team drew a number six, and their car was sixth in the row behind the peloton. Well, it was actually eighth, as there are still the Tour Radio, mobile radio station vehicle, and the doctor's car in front of the number one, maybe even the odd commissaire.

Number one indicates the best starting position in the caravan

There's even more metal on the wheels in front of the peloton – the race director, race official, neutral vehicle, press vehicle, a plethora of cameras, and the police. But let's get back to behind the peloton, where the team vehicles are. If someone from the yellow bunch needs it, sixth place is a good starting point from which it can hurry to help. And then, a surprise happens – Jumbo-Visma's Mike Teunissen wins the stage in a sprint finish so tight that it has to be confirmed by a photo finish. That means he now leads the GC standings and wears the yellow jersey, and that the number 1 will be stuck on the rear window of the first Jumbo-Visma's team vehicle that will lead the caravan. The first vehicle, because each team has two: many times one has to follow the breakaway.

An example of such situation could have been observed during the Giro in 2019, when Primož won, and therefore the following day his team car was allocated the number 1. We will have a closer look at the way the team cars follow their riders in a time trial a little bit later.

In short, the vehicles follow the riders according to the placement of their best rider in the general classification. This is how the Vuelta GC

looked after five stages:
1. LOPEZ MORENO, Miguel Angel (ASTANA PRO)
2. ROGLIČ, Primož (JUMBO-VISMA)
3. QUINTANA, Nairo (MOVISTAR)
4. VALVERDE, Alejandro (MOVISTAR)

The car with the number 1 was Astana's. The second in the row was ours. Movistar had the number 3. A million-dollar question – who had the number 4? Not Alejandro; he shared a vehicle with Quintana. It was Sunweb's car, as their Nicolas Roche was in fifth place in the general classification.

Why did I say that the Tour started with a regular stage? We know already that if the race begins with a prologue or a time trial, every rider has his vehicle behind him. I mean his team car, not the one from his home garage. When it comes to time trial, every car has a magnetic plate with the rider's name and starting number.

If something happens and a mechanic is required, he will jump out of the car, take the spare bike from the roof, and help the rider start riding again. Then he'll take the damaged bike and continue to follow the rider in the car.

Sometimes it can take quite a while, and the rider falls behind by a lot. Riders who crashed sometimes draft behind the vehicles, which is not allowed. The race commissaire may even disqualify a rider over that. It often happens that riders return to the peloton in the motorcade – that means they needed a lot of time before they could carry on, and they simply had no other choice but to ride behind and among vehicles.

Nameplates with riders' numbers: these are attached to team cars during the time trial

The other very well-known and also forbidden method of sly cheating is a so-called sticky bottle. The rider drops back to the team vehicle to get a drink and holds on to the water bottle being passed to him through the window. The car pulls him along. In the event of very brief contact, commissars generally tolerate such behavior, but they can (and they probably will) sanction it, punishing the rider and his DS for exploiting it.

An escort motorbike, a rider, and a team car during a time trial

Those badly hurt in a crash who continue to race can seek help by the medical car. Because riders are not just somewhat »special« but also very resilient, the medical staff treats their wounds through the car window while they keep riding. Who could forget the Giro 2019 scene when Primož, wearing the pink jersey, showed his backside for all the world to see after crashing, as the doctor took care of his wound. He was holding on to the car, which is allowed.

Commissars tend to turn a blind eye for mechanical failures too. When it comes to that, the unfortunate rider drops back to the team car, where he may change his bike or make a repair on the go if the mechanical failure is not too bad. The mechanic leans through the back window and tries to fix the problem if possible. In the meantime, the rider is holding on to the car.

> **"** *I have no idea what the rules are if you have a puncture and stay behind. Your car is not allowed to tow you, but other team cars can – or something like that. The fight is not considered to be fair if someone had bad luck.* **"**

We got to know another jersey in this stage – the best young rider is awarded a white one. The Tour of Spain includes riders up to 25 years of age in this category and awards the white jersey to the best young rider in the general classification. Lopez was the leader in this classification, but he was also the GC leader, so he wore the red jersey. Tadej Pogačar was second in the best young rider classification, so he wore the white jersey on Lopez's behalf.

The peloton communicates with a unique vocabulary. If technological advances ever allow microphones on all riders' handlebars – kind of like microphones on tennis nets – we'll be able to hear fascinating conversations. But we're not that far yet, and we'll have to make do with occasional recordings from cameras that randomly chosen riders have underneath their saddle or handlebars. In the last kilometers, we mostly hear them screaming: »Right, left, brake, go!« It sure looks as panicky as it sounds.

But riders mostly communicate with hands. They bring obstacles to the attention of the riders behind them or declare their next move. For instance, when a rider decides to ride out of the saddle, he'll let the rider behind him know by flicking his hands open on both sides while still holding on to the handlebars with his thumbs. Or he'll move his elbows as if doing the funky chicken dance. A rider who might be only three centimeters behind will know about a sudden change of rhythm and will be able to predict the movements in front of him, reducing the chance of a crash.

THE BEGINNING OF THE JOURNEY

Ljubljana, August 29, 2019

We finally drove off. I have no idea what happened during the stage because I was running up and down the stairs like a headless chicken trying to cram the baby's stuff into the camper. A classic with a small difference. And yes, that difference is tiny, but very loud and bossy. What do I know about packing for a two-month-old mini human for a trip to Spain? With a mobile home? To a race? I don't even know how to pack for a walk in the park without forgetting something. The stress of such departures was always bad enough even without a baby when the cans of barley soup and kitchenware came flying out of the drawers at the camper's first move.

We're late anyway; water is leaking, apples are rolling around the floor, the little one is screaming, take this and take that, and also that, you never know, we may need it. Or we might not.

Apparently, there was an ugly crash in the race, and Rigo already went home. Luckily my man wasn't in it. He finished at the same time as all the important GCers; only Superman[35] was a bit faster.

The camper almost got stuck in the corner when we drove off the front yard. This will be fun. They say Spanish roads are not like French ones; if you're lucky, you can drag yourself with a huge vehicle up a hill or two in France. The Pyrenees excluded. The little one flew half a meter in the air at the first speed bump, shocking him into being quiet all the way to the first rest stop and forcing me to start wondering if this was really such a good idea.

And I admit I'm scared a little. But I can't afford not to go. On the other hand, the unknown is very exciting for me – not knowing how it will go, if at all. It will be cool, and if Lev and I manage to reach Madrid, it will be a victory in and of itself. Let's go; the road is straight and inviting. The Vuelta is calling.

---

[35] Lopez's nickname.

STAGE SEVEN

AUGUST 30, 2019

ONDA ·······→ MAS DE LA COSTA

183 KM, MOUNTAIN

ONLY THE WORLD CHAMPION IN FRONT OF ROGLIČ AT THE TOP OF THE SWEET HELL

[_] Only four elite riders remained at the front in the wild finish climb at
Mas de La Costa in stage seven of the Vuelta, and only 39-year old Alejandro
Valverde was stronger than Primož Roglič. [_]

The world champion Valverde (Movistar) proved that age is not an obstacle. He
picked up the pace 150 meters before the finish line, and only Roglič (Jumbo-
Visma) was able to follow, though he didn't manage to catch the veteran, who is
riding his 28th Grand Tour (he won the Vuelta in 2009). [_] The finish climb was
only 4.1 kilometers long but challenging; the average grade was 12.3 percent
with two sections inclining more than 20 percent. [_]

Miguel Angel Lopez donned the red jersey again after Dylan Teuns fell behind on
the last climb and couldn't keep up with the punishing pace of team Movistar and
lost almost ten minutes in the end. Roglič praised **his teammates for their help**.
[_] (RTV MMC 2019f)

COL 1. LOPEZ MORENO, MIGUEL ANGEL (ASTANA PRO)   28:19:13

SLO 2. ROGLIČ, PRIMOŽ (JUMBO-VISMA)   +6

ESP 3. VALVERDE, ALEJANDRO (MOVISTAR)   +16

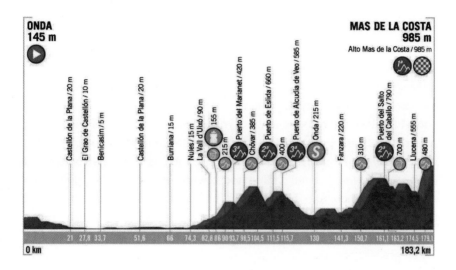

Is there anything interesting on this profile except the almost vertical climb at the end? Why the hell is a trash can there?

Riders will start riding with pockets full of food. When they reach the first trash can, where you can also see a sign for a water bottle, their pockets will be empty. They will have eaten most of their food by then. With cycling being a sport considerate of the environment, the trash can (also signposted on the actual course) indicates the designated area where riders may toss their trash – we'll call that area a waste zone or a green zone. Contrary to the waste zone, where riders empty their pockets, the feed zone is where they fill them again.

On this profile, it's marked with a water bottle, but on some others, it shows a crossed fork and knife even though riders don't have time for a proper lunch in the feed zone. Almost for the entire race, the riders may be seen dropping back to their team car for some food. Why dropping back? Because the car is behind the peloton. We'll see later who they send there and why. In the first 30 and the last 20 kilometers, fetching food and drinks is not allowed. As an unwritten rule, there should also be no attacking in the feed zone.

Lunch during a race is most similar to riding your bike to the McDonald's Drive-thru. Of course, they won't stop while they're eating. There will be *soigneurs* waiting by the side of the road in the feed zone, with little, long-handled linen bags called *musettes* – another distinguishing characteristic of cycling. Before they check the contents of the bag, riders hang it over their body. Inside, they'll probably find a water bottle and an isotonic drink, a small caffeinated beverage, energy bars, gels, even a small sandwich, and a rice cake, which is rice mixed with something sweet. Everything is bite-sized. The capacity to take in enormous amounts of food in a very short time is another fascinating trait shared by all professional riders.

In short, riders will pull out of the bag only things they want and they'll throw away the rest, including the bag – that's why the green zone is an area where everything flies through the air, and you would be well advised to mind your head.

You probably won't find a job advertisement for a *soigneur*. The swannies, as the peloton calls them lovingly, are jacks-of-all-trades. French is the language of cycling, and in French, a *soigneur* means a servant – with no negative connotation.

We don't do them justice if we say they're masseurs. A *soigneur* is an indispensable member of the team – he'll drag the bags from the hotel rooms to the bus in the morning, boil rice for the race, mix drinks and fill water bottles, and wait with lunch in the feed zone. He'll wait for his riders with dry clothes and a recovery drink at the finish, help them take off their shoes, and wipe the muck off their face before they step onto the podium. He'll wash their dirty clothes and massage them before dinner. A rider may send him to the store to buy a toothbrush he forgot to bring from home or ask him to make some shade for him while he spins his legs on a trainer.

Riders going for lunch

That is one more indicator that cycling is a team sport. A team always comes to the race with a specific goal in mind. They may want to win as many stages as possible, or they may want to win the general classification. They may be interested only in sprint stages because they have an excellent sprinter and a lead-out train, or they may have ambitions in the mountains.

These things get decided as essential points long before the race, because of the type of riders the team leader wants by his side.

The team aiming for sprint wins will do everything to fulfill the needs of its best sprinter. When he has the best possible support of his teammates, he'll be able to do his part in his best capacity.

We won't see any skinny guys who excel in climbing up the steepest climbs in such teams. They will be in teams that want to win the GC. Teams can also combine riders. To the TDF, they might send one sprinter with three comrades, who will slingshot from the roundabout in the last kilometer at 80 km/h to give Dylan[36] the best possible position in the finish. Besides them, they can also send a GC rider, let's say Primož, with three domestiques who are strong climbers. But this is always a risky move. Three riders is not that many, and it can quickly happen that one of them withdraws, another has a bad day, and you can easily find yourself all alone.

Some teams are aware that they don't stand a chance of significant accomplishments and participate in a given race just to try to make an impact in the breakaway and proudly show off their sponsors on live TV.

Cycling is a team sport. That may sound strange as there's only one guy on the podium in the end. A team with ambitions for a good result in the

Cycling is a team sport

---

[36] Dylan Groenewegen, an excellent Dutch sprinter and Primož's teammate at Jumbo-Visma.

general classification meticulously divvies up its riders' roles. Everything revolves around the team leader.

Let's say we're interested in the Jumbo-Visma team racing in the Vuelta. We know the team leader; it's Primož Roglič. His teammates' primary job is to make his work easier, to help him, and that's why they're called domestiques. Their roles are assigned based on their individual strong suits. Four-time time trial world champion Tony Martin can't really help him in the mountains. Riders of his kind will protect him on the flats, in windy conditions, and in the peloton while trying to find a favorable position on the road. They will control the breakaway and dictate the tempo in the bunch, as well as defend their position in front of it.

In theory, domestiques will always be somewhere close, if not right by their leader's side in the ideal scenario. They'll try to bring him to the best position possible and protect him from crashes that occur because of contacts with other riders; a tiny touch of wheels is enough to take down half of the peloton. Domestique is the most commonly used name for helpers in cycling. Sometimes, but rarely, they're also called water boys because they occasionally have to drop back to the rear of the peloton to get a drink, food, and of course, water. The Italians call them *gregario*. A super domestique is a better version of a domestique, and he can happen to be even better than the team leader, but the roles are very clear. There have been many times when a domestique had to literally stop before the finish line. However, because races are unpredictable, the roles can change in the event of injuries, illness, or due to some other reason.

Nevertheless, this is honorable work. Real domestiques will always do their best to make their leader's life as comfortable as possible. They will grab his musette in the feed zone; they will help him when nature calls – boys pee without getting of the bike[37]. If they take a leak in the wrong place, forbidden by the UCI, for instance, where there are many

---

[37] The team leader is the boss even when it comes to answering the call of nature. He pees while riding with a teammate pushing him along so he doesn't have to stop.

spectators, a fine will follow. Fines are dished out for many reasons. In the notification letter, peeing will be referred to as indecent exposure. Criminals!

Domestiques always keep an eye on their leader; they also talk over the radio if they can't do it in person.

But first and foremost, their job is to control the race and maintain a very high pace to prevent attacks and make a selection, as it happened in this stage.

By dictating the tempo, they make sure that as few other riders as possible keep up – the fewer domestiques other team leaders have, the better for us. If one or two team leaders also happen to get dropped, the work was done very well. If a team leader has a domestique or two left towards the end of the stage, they can take turns attacking. If another team's leader remains alone, his life can get miserable quickly, as he has to neutralize all attacks himself. The more rivals' attacks domestiques cover, the more energy for the final move the team leader conserves. If we speak of a neutralized attack, it means that someone upped their pace and gained a few meters on others, but then a member of our team caught up with him and is now on his back wheel, breathing down his neck – that's the moment the attack was stopped. The later the team leader is isolated, the better.

A team leader can also send his domestiques into a breakaway in some stages. This is easier said than done, but the feeling of having one of your own riders in front is good. It's also convenient to have domestiques by your side if you have a mechanical or a crash. Such equipment exchange is much faster than when having to wait for your team vehicle.

As far as domestiques are concerned, a good personal result is rarely their goal, as they must watch out for their leader most of the time. That means they'll cross the finish line far behind even if they're in their top form. For most of them, a time trial stage where their leader has a good chance of winning is more or less a rest day because they have to conserve their energy for the upcoming days.

Something is clear – the whole team must work as one to reach top results in the end.

The leader has to behave like a battalion commander off the road, too, because he's the first among equals. The unwritten rule says that the winner of a Grand Tour relinquishes his part of the prize money. Every stage win, GC win, day in the leader's jersey, point, etc., is measured in Euros. At the end, the organizers add up everything the team accumulated over the past three weeks and distribute the money equally to all the riders in the winner's team.

Let's say the Jumbo-Visma team earned a hundred thousand Euros in the Vuelta. The money was shared among the riders and staff, while Primož relinquished his part. After attaining a big win, the leader habitually gives some gifts to his teammates, who fought for him on the road. These gifts are usually of significant value – tablets, vacation, wristwatches, coffee machines, scooters, etc.

SHORT, SWEET

Foix, a weird place before the beginning of the hill that leads to Andorra, August 30, 2019

I don't know if I would even reflect on the fact that, after a whole night of driving and debating about how we should absolutely never ever stop, let alone spend a night south of Cannes (because the south of France is quite dangerous), we stopped precisely there.

We hid in a corner behind a truck, which didn't stop me from hanging on the window nevertheless. Just to be on the safe side, I also checked the location on my cell, in case I had to call the special units, pompiers, or gendarmes. I mean – what! The little progeny was having sweet dreams, as if he couldn't care less of any of my troubles. After a while, I got fed up staring through the window because, luckily, there was no ninja to be seen anywhere. I just plopped myself to the side of the little man and dozed off for a few minutes.

We resumed our journey alive and well at six o'clock. Close to Narbonne, at a much fancier rest area, we threw away the dirty diapers, and France greeted us with a croissant and the gentle spilling of the sun over the landscape.

A few dozen kilometers later, my mother Patricija, whom we finally entrusted with a steering wheel, remembers she was here in maybe 1977 when she was still in primary school.

»I'm sure it was here, some kind of a national park. And what a beautiful beach, you know,« Patricija, the driver, continues her monologue.

»And there was some kind of swamp, and also white horses,« I keep listening, increasingly irritated, sitting at the table behind her. »Hey, are you sure you have never seen a commercial for Champagne? Because that's up there, at the top.«

My pro and I drove all over France in the last couple of years looking for and studying all kinds of technical intricacies and mysteries of the climbs and country cart roads that might get included in the race. Most of the time, without speaking and in different vehicles. The electric tension of our dia-

logues, in which I was mostly to blame for the roadblocks and he for the phone not working, sooner or later turned into frantic gesticulating through the car window or angry gestures on the bike. I would mostly see his flapping about in the rearview mirror while I would be muttering into the steering wheel: »Like if I care about you or your damn bike. As far as I am concerned, you can stay where you are and figure it out with your bonjouuuur.«

Everything went wrong as soon as mom mentioned the beach. I reckon Vinko has a special filter in his ears that detects that word. I'm just waiting for someone to suggest we stop there. And everyone's all for it, of course!

I start rolling my eyes even before that happens. It's hot as hell, so this is the last thing I need now. We stop, what else! The beach is long and wide, but we can't get to it. The camper gets stuck under the branches in a narrow alley, and precisely at that moment, a Frenchman, burnt to a crisp, runs around the corner and starts furiously nagging at me. I'm pointing to the baby, like shut up, dude, we'll only be like half an hour, the little one is burning with heat.

I'm dragging my feet like a drama queen, kicking the sand up to my knees and desperately trying to get everyone to notice the vein on my forehead popping out in protest, but no one pays attention to me. Everyone runs for the sea as if they've never seen it before.

Sand is flying everywhere, even before we get to the water. Somewhere in the distance is Perpignan, where we will leave the sea and turn right, towards the mountains.

Sand must have about five hundred degrees. Lev goes berserk and screams at the top of his lungs, for real, when they soak his feet in the water. No wonder; this is pure torture, and I'd blow a fuse, too, because, Jesus Christ, I'm really not made for the sea. So what, kill me! I'm not going in.

Since we are already talking about them, the water-obsessed people. With seawater, make no mistake, because freshwater fish are stupid – in case you didn't know. »Hello?! Carps eat shit from the riverbed,« Vinko would have us know. His real name is Dominik, and he's my brother. Let *me confirm my statement by telling you he read Hamlet for his graduation exam in a wetsuit.*

I can hardly wait to get to the thin air. I don't know how many hours and kilometers later we stop at a store with a parking big enough to welcome us, and here we are. I cut the trouser legs of my old jeans off, feeling they'll become my good friends on this trip.

There are hills everywhere. Where exactly am I supposed to find a fuse for the fridge here? I'm dragging myself from one store to the next, showing the blown yellow fuse. »Pour le frigo,« I keep asking, and anxiety slowly creeps in because today's stage of the Vuelta ends with a real bombshell, a short but sweet steep climb. The kind he loves, I think to myself. Valverde, too. And many others.

The bloody antenna, squeezed among the hills, doesn't want to work. Finally, we get the German Eurosport, and of course, the picture freezes in the last kilometer. What? What happened?

He was just a tad short; he came in second. And Alejandro is really a master of these kinds of climbs. Great. Take the antenna down, and let's move on.

The road takes us by the sign for Font-Romeu. Why does it seem so familiar to me? On a gentle pass with ruins of some kind of a fortress and green grass that looks so soft, we fill the tank up. The gasoline is almost free. The view spilling over the valleys is majestic.

There's a pizza machine in front of a building that is nearly hanging off the edge and looks like a forgotten hotel. It's the first time I've seen anything like it. A tin box by the solitary road that actually puts together a pizza and bakes it?

Then I remember. Font-Romeu is a Pyrenean base for the altitude training for the boys from the peloton. Like CAR[38] in the Sierra Nevada. I google it. It opened in 1967 at 1850 meters when French athletes came here to prepare for the Olympic games of 1968 in Mexico City. The summer Olympics had never before been held at such an altitude – at 2240 meters.

---

[38] Centro de Alto Rendimiento – a top notch sports center at 2320 meters above sea level.

Uncle Vinko (well, Dominik) hard at work

STAGE EIGHT

AUGUST 31, 2019

VALLS ·······▶ IGUALADA

167 KM, HILLY

ARNDT THE STRONGEST IN THE BREAKAWAY BATTERED BY RAIN - EDET TAKES THE RED JERSEY

The bunch with all the favorites crossed the finish line more than nine minutes behind. Nikias Arndt was the strongest in the breakaway of the 8th stage of the Tour of Spain. The bunch followed over nine minutes later, which means Nicolas Edet took the red jersey. [...]

The peloton crossed the finish line more than nine minutes after Arndt. The two best Slovenians in the general classification, Primož Roglič, and Tadej Pogačar, who wore the best young rider's white jersey instead of Miguel Angel Lopez today, were in front. Astana's leader relinquished the GC lead after only one day for the third time in this Vuelta. [...] (RTV MMMC 2019g)

```
FRA 1. EDET, NICOLAS (COFIDIS, SOLUTIONS CREDITS)      32:16:24
BEL 2. TEUNS, DYLAN (BAHRAIN-MERIDA)                      +2:21
COL 3. LOPEZ MORENO, MIGUEL ANGEL (ASTANA PRO)           +3:01
SLO 4. ROGLIČ, PRIMOŽ (JUMBO-VISMA)                      +3:07
```

The boys in the peloton obviously established no one in the break-away posed a threat, and the escape was good to go, so they let them go. And, judging by the weather, they surely used a rain bag. What is that?

> ❝ *If it's cold and very wet, it's not fun. That's when we send someone to fetch the rain rags from the team vehicle. Every rider has a so-called* borsa per freddo. *Actually, not one, but two – one in each car. It's literally a bag for cold weather. There's everything but the kitchen sink inside, spare shoes, a bunch of gloves, a jacket, all kinds of overshoes, gilets. Overshoes are an overlay for shoes, and even though they're supposed to be warm and waterproof, after ten minutes in heavy rain, you're soaking wet. In Vuelta, I usually asked for a thicker rain jacket with short sleeves.* ❞

Rain bag

POMMA

Andorra, the last Saturday of August 2019

I can't believe my shitty luck. Like a mother cat that grabs her kitten close to its tail and carries it around, we, I, with my two months old, drove across half of Europe, through 5698 tunnels, three times over Mount Everest, and now an angry female cop, who can't even fart a word of English, spits with that Spanish S at me that I can't go to the top of the hill – just because. No room. A bit further on, someone else tells me the same, and now, even more furious, I'm trying to figure out what that clown even said.

It's so steep the camper almost breaks in half, yet the big boss makes us park the camper just six kilometers from the top. And even that is just for tonight; tomorrow we have to bug off, because the carrera *is going through here. I glance at the parking lot, looking for a Porsche. Yes, I know, she meant the race!*

I'm fuming. I'm fuming. I'm about to burst into flames. The night crawls over humongous climbs. Faithful to our tradition, we have an overture fight with pots flying. We just can't start without it; presumably, the rest of the week will be peaceful after that.

The next morning is beautiful. Vinko and dad have to go over »Mont Blanc« to get a SIM card; without it, we don't have any contact with the outside world, no information whatsoever, because Andorra is a special place, belonging to no one. As if a part of the Pyrenees was to be squeezed between France and Spain, but there was no room, resulting in meters of flat we can count on one hand. And even those are artificial, a mountain upon mountain lowering to a hill upon hill, just like on those 3D greeting cards.

For the first time in more than a year, I sit on a bike. Every rider will tell you that you feel every forgotten part of your body on the first ride after a long time. I'm riding. How cool, I'm riding. There's a lake three kilometers away. Gravel is grinding beneath the bike, and views open up where magnificent

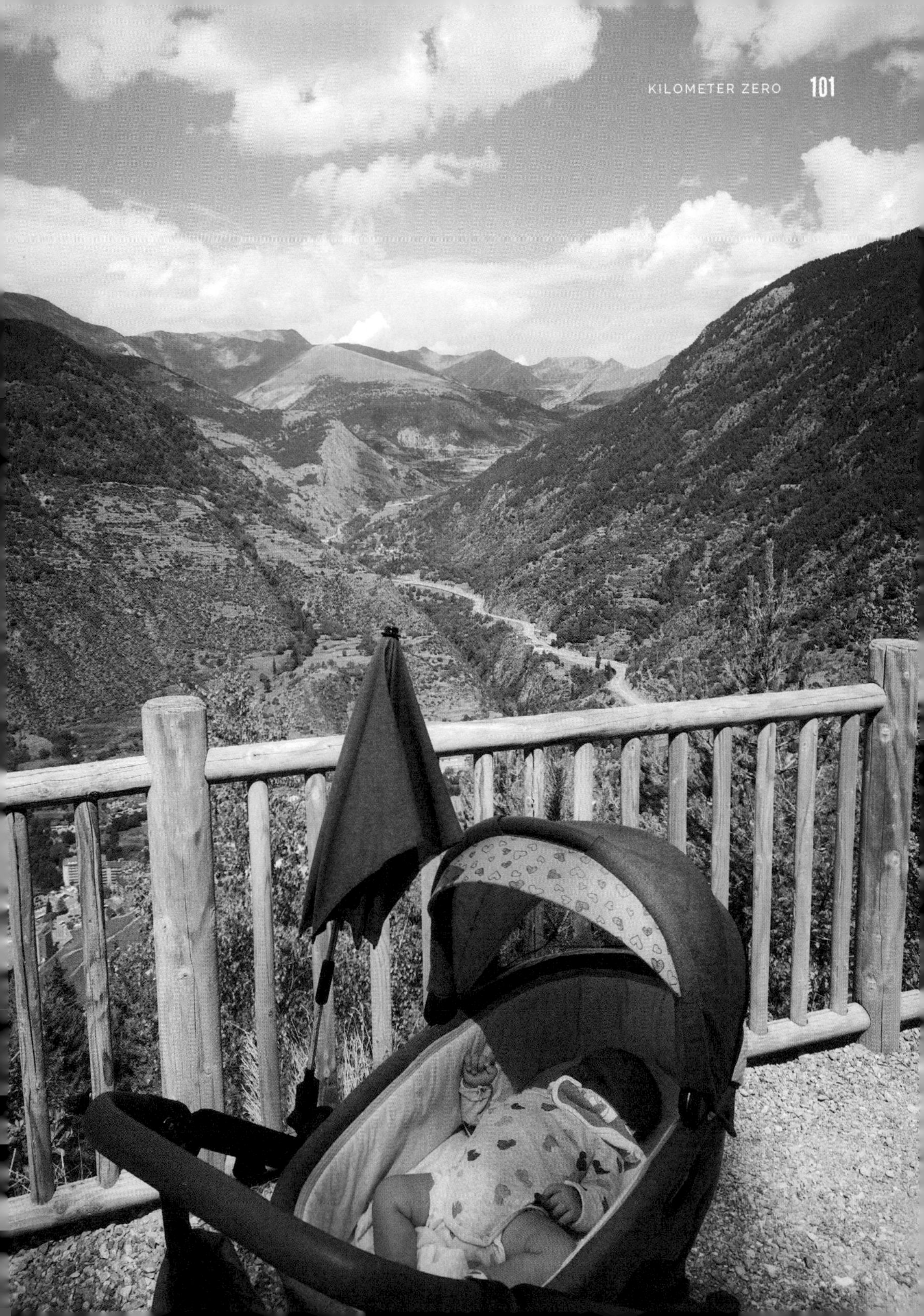

roads in the distance snake over mountains. Mountains and mountains and chasms. There's probably a very similar view behind the next mountain. Villages are just miniscule brown piles in the distance – I only saw wooden hotels by the road.

Bridges, streams, green water, tunnels carved into rocks. The green color of the lake blends in with the soft green grass, people are reading books, life is beautiful.

There's a kind of an exhibition in the woods a bit further, where sculptures are hanging from trees. And at the end of the lake, there's a skyrocketing summit that ends as soon as it begins. From the top, the view extends over another valley, over more mountains. In the bottom of the valley there are tight rows of campers, which I find odd. I frown to myself, huh. That seems really weird. I turn back. Then, I notice arrows on trees, much like those used to show riders the way. Lora, you missed something.

Oh my god! A light bulb flashes over my head like in a cartoon, and it dawns on me. The race goes through here. It goes through here before it turns onto the main road to Cortals d'Encamp. Ahaaaaa!

Delighted, I descend back, I need to tell someone. The race goes through here! Trying to create a spectacle, they're pushing the riders' safety to the very edge. They had gravel sections in the Tour this year and in the Giro last year. There will be a crazy amount of flats here. And that is, at the very top of the curve, after a whole day of screwing with endless hills, it's entirely possible that you'll get stuck six kilometers from the finish line with a flat tire. Oh, this will be fun.

Before we stuff back everything we dragged out of our camper, the sun is already pushing behind the jagged horizon. There's an abnormal amount of stuff. I know it will be challenging to find a spot for our trailer on the evening before the race. I'm trying to follow the signs, but the language is stiff and weird, kind of a hacked, hilly Catalan. Andorrans are such complicators. I never studied Spanish, but through the years I've heard so many ques and buenosdiases *that it's anchored itself somewhere deep inside me, and I've understood it very well on occasions.*

But not always. When we came to Girona years ago, I made a beeline to the store with my head full of mulled-over handbooks, like Speaking Spanish in Two Months, Spanish for Dummies, etc. I almost had a stroke when I saw that apples were not labeled manzana, *as I had been repeating to myself for two days, but* pomma. *Q-u-e? When I first came into contact with Catalan, French was my savior. The two are much more similar – pomme is French for apple.*

A year later, while looking for new climbs and a mild Spanish winter, we spent most of the time on Mallorca. A beautiful island, but they speak a kind of gibberish there, which is called Mallorquin. I didn't even try to find a connection with anything remotely speakable. After that, I was fed up with Spain.

And now, after a few years in the Pyrenees, I've bumped into that funny gobbledygook once again. Whatever the language, the feeling that we're at the scene of a magnificent event that will undoubtedly shape the future, near future for sure, is calming yet exciting at the same time. The little man is in the corner of the bed, tucked in like the Princess and the Pea, while the rest of the crew are using every limb available to hold the bike and pots and pans in place while the camper heads down the road. I might just like you yet, Andorra.

STAGE NINE

SEPTEMBER 1, 2019

ANDORRA LA VELLA ·······▶ CORTALS D'ENCAMP

94 KM, MOUNTAIN

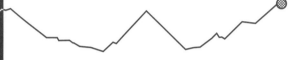

INCREDIBLE POGAČAR WINS THE QUEEN STAGE IN ANDORRA, ROGLIČ LAYS THE RED FOUNDATION

Quintana in the red jersey. Tadej Pogačar is the hero of the queen stage of the Tour of Spain. The 20-year-old was the strongest rider on the summit finish to Cortals d'Encamp. Primož Roglič struggled at the bottom of the climb but managed to recover and finished third.

Only a 94.4-kilometer-long stage with five categorized climbs produced a battle of the best riders of the world, but Pogačar crushed them all to finish off the last climb of the day. The youngest rider in this year's edition of the Tour of Spain followed Nairo Quintana's attack. When the Columbian got the help of his then leading teammate, Spaniard Marc Soler, the 20-year-old rode ahead and celebrated his career's biggest success so far. […]

Quintana finished 23 seconds behind Pogačar and took the red jersey. Roglič was third, crossing the finish line 48 seconds behind Pogačar, and is now second in the general classification. The leader of team Jumbo-Visma is in a great position, being only six seconds behind with a 36-kilometer time trial coming up on Tuesday. […]

Roglič found himself in trouble in the middle of a very challenging stage but managed to recover with the help of his teammates Robert Gesink and Sepp Kuss. The American revealed that the rider from Zasavje crashed on the gravel section when he tried to avoid one of the motorbikes, consequently lost touch with his group, and had to chase them down. […] (RTV MMC 2019h)

COL	1. QUINTANA, NAIRO (MOVISTAR)	35:18:18
SLO	2. ROGLIČ, PRIMOŽ (JUMBO-VISMA)	+6
COL	3. LOPEZ MORENO, MIGUEL ANGEL (ASTANA PRO)	+17

To summarize, we can add a motorbike rider standing behind the wall at the inner side of the corner, on a gravel section, in an apocalyptic hailstorm to the list of other crash causes. Never, ever stand on the inside of the corner, because riders will always choose the shorter route. The motorcyclist helped put the chain back on, but the rivals were already a long way off.

We've also seen a situation involving Quintana's teammate in the lead. He wasn't far off the finish line, but was ordered to wait for his team leader. The Spaniard was livid. And Pogačar grabbed the opportunity with both hands.

APOCALYPSE

Andorra, September 1, 2019

Besides us, there is another camper, a bus, and the Vuelta organizer's vehicle in the parking lot. When I was staring through the window, I realized people were bringing their dogs to pee here. Encamp, a forgotten town in Andorra. There are very few people here and, if they're not locals, they're here for the same reason we are. It was cold in the morning – nothing strange, if you're in the most mountainous principality ever. Today, que será, será. Queen stage? A bit higher I can see some kind of a cable car that will supposedly take people to the summit.

The stage is short, and it will start late. In the morning, Primož will go for a quick spot of training – I told you riders are weird. Their accommodation is near the start, while we're sitting in the valley under the last climb like some kind of sediment at the bottom of a glass. When he says he'll ride to us before the start, I feel butterflies in my stomach as if I were freshly in love.

I only spot him when I hear people by the main road clapping and cheering. Are they clapping for him? He's going the wrong way, I yell from the edge of the parking lot. I see he has his starting number under the saddle, and after more than two weeks, we're a bit closer to each other. When he rides up to the camper, the little hedgehog, wrapped in everything his bag carries, just stares at him suspiciously. Even though yesterday's sunset was glorious when we were teasing the Spaniards in a true Balkan manner (the parking lot was supposed to be empty at 18.00, yet I was still posing for photos by the fence at 17:57), I must admit it would be even colder up there on the mountain.

Thanks to an app – highlight of technological advancement - we have found a parking lot for campers in the middle of town. We also have to thank my dad and Vinko, who both sacrificed themselves, especially their legs and lungs, and descended to the valley to get a SIM card. With fingers crossed, because you can never trust technology completely, we held onto the pots and the child while the camper crawled downhill into the civilization.

The victorious yellow one teared up when he saw his offspring, wrapped up like a sprained ankle, and I teared up when I saw him looking at the little man. Such fleeting reunions are always ... Maybe you wish for them, but maybe you'd rather not have them. He must hurry to the start line, and it would be good for him to focus. So I tell him to go already. When he says he came over the mountain pass, I feel like I've ruined the Vuelta. I start to worry – what if he ran out of legs, and so on.

On the other hand, I'm over the moon to see him, and I'm thinking about locking him up behind the water tank and letting him out only when we pass Madrid. I find

Quick visit before the queen stage

it incredibly sweet that he came to see us in a situation like this, before the queen stage, that there is part within him that is not only about his bike. He even cycled over the mountain pass! So he would get that final bit of encouragement. Assurance and belief that we'll still be here no matter what – even if he fucks up. He's already in his zone - Primož, the rider, but with us he remains gentle. I should beat him up for not going through the tunnel. I really can't understand him having such an urge to drag himself over the climbs, especially with a multitude of hills waiting for him in the afternoon.

And then, clipping in with one shoe, he sort of half turns on his saddle in his typical way. **"** *Don't go up there. Stay here. They're expecting pandemonium.* **"**

I pretend to be indifferent. I've learned it by now, on days, when he is at the breaking point, there is no room for my shit.

»You think?« I ask sourly and add an »okay.« A shrug and he's off while I miserably sit back behind the folding table by the bus that's, oh, the irony, going to Girona where we lived during his first pro season. In my socks and sandals, while he is disappearing on the horizon. Metaphorically, I feel like chasing rainbows – again. I have a frog in my throat, and my eyes are welling up with tears. I can't get stuck six kilometers from the finish line after I've driven almost two thousand kilometers to get here. Of course, I'll go up there! He'll never know. »Listen to him if he said not to go up. Lora, you know, he has a good nose for that kind of stuff.«

I have a good nose, too – so what! I'm banging my mug against the camper, as if I was drinking vinegar from a jar of pickles rather than coffee. I can't afford to stay below. No, no, no! I'll never forgive myself. I go to the other side of the camper and look up. The sky is blue. What storm is he talking about? I fold my arms.

I'll go, and come what may. I scour the internet for weather information about Andorra on the one phone that is working. Realization that man's will is insignificant against the most magnificent Pyrenees giants brings a lump to my throat. The phone says it won't be surprising if the steep, pathless slopes get covered by snow. In August. I'll chuck you into the ravine if you don't stop this nonsensical prognosis, I utter at the phone through my teeth. I really will, I think to myself. Then I decide – no. You were lucky this time, you lying piece of junk.

My family votes against me going to the top, especially with the mini-man; a conspiracy against me! You're all against it; you, who are all going up, and I'm supposed to stay here? »Listen to him, he's usually right,« blah, blah, blah, go to hell the lot of you!

In the end, I stay put, brokenhearted, and deflated. I don't even want to say goodbye; I don't feel like talking. It's not fair. The pass reader is buzzing, they're entering the gondola, my eyes are welling up with tears, my throat is closing, and I'm looking away as I can't bear to look at these traitors. But on the other hand, I'm insisting they have to go to the finish area. It feels like

I'm sending my envoys to do my work for me. The sun is still shining, and I'm still shaking my head in disbelief, wounded.

As empty cable cars swing on a thick cable above the main road, I know it's over. I'm stuck at the bottom. I came to the Vatican, but I didn't get to see the pope.

The base cable car station is like a house of horrors, there is one and a half souls left – me and the mini-man. The team bus of Not-Primož's team picks us up in the middle of the road. Three guys jump out of the narrow door like some kind of special forces, and Lev's stroller flies up the steep steps while a cop is having a fit behind the exhaust pipe.

I have never seen anything like it. We park by the road and wait. Two TV sets, air conditioning at full blast, we are eating and drinking; the guys are due to hit the gravel soon. Teeth clenched, it's the moment of truth; I just hope he doesn't get a puncture or something along that line.

Tick, tock, the TV blacks out, and we look at each other in silence. The screen is an impenetrable blackness without any signs of life. Only after a while, we find out there's sleet, even hail. There's no TV signal; the antennas probably took a good beating. I can't believe I'm drinking Dom Perignon on a bus where alcohol is strictly forbidden, while those poor guys are grinding it outside, battered by an icy attack from the heavens. Idiot as I am, I needed quite a while to figure out what they are referring to as »dompe«.

I look outside. The blue among the mountains, I don't know when, turned black. Sharp peaks in the distance ominously loom above us, and the sky is pressing down with all its force. The picture emerges on the screen precisely at the moment they leave the gravel. We hear the clanking of the ice on metal, mixed with hoarse commentary on the TV. There's nobody in yellow there. Shit. Maybe we would be a bit in their way with a camper if we were there. And then the camera finds him; he's alone. Luckily I can't see his face well. The look of being at the end of the rope that emerges in his eyes always hurts me. What can I do? We can only wait for the race to unravel. I pretend not to be nervous, even though sweat trickles down my back almost to my ankles. The guys on the bus are speaking in Italian. »He will catch them,« says someone. Because he said it in English, I figure it was meant for me.

We cheer as attacks start coming; Lev is startled and starts to roar like a lion. I'm stuffing the bottle into his mouth, but he doesn't want it. I swear I'll go berserk. The kid wants my tit, not the bottle. »And you just have to do this now, for Christ's sake!«

I have to move into the rear end of the bus, into the corner with helmets of some Grand Tour winners hanging from a shelf. And not only he wants my tit; to top it all, he crapped himself. And I can't see the TV from this corner.

Pogi wins, Primi catches up with them, and there's a horrendous storm at the top that is slowly creeping over us too. The yellow psychic was right

Battle for the gondola

again. I'm rolling my eyes, already thinking about his endless " I told you so, didn't I." *The point is undeniable; he was right again, and I'll just have to admit it through my gritted teeth when I see him. Oh, and where did I get to see him?*

Let's say the bus is parked about a kilometer from the base station of the gondola. There's a terrible storm, merciless intervals of rain are changing from pouring to pouring even more. I'm wet through and through as I try to protect my cub from drowning in his stroller. We're running along the road, stopping occasionally because Mattia knows everyone. At some point, we buy an umbrella and so on, until the sequence of events brings us into the gondola station at the precise moment when an angry yellow one steps out of a cable car. Going by his body language, pacing with long steps up and down, wrapping his arms tightly around himself, he must be freezing. Regardless, when he sees us, he manages to squeeze out a smile.

The three traitors are five steps behind him, wearing soaking wet raincoats that stretch to the floor. They look like crushed jellyfish as they tell me that they ran into Primož, who was almost crawling on all fours over a steep, pathless, grassy slope to return from the hill with the gondola as quickly as possible. He dragged them into his cable car. There were only riders in there. And three soaked jellyfish from Hoče.

So, even though I was expecting to hear "I told you so" *instead of hello, he spits out angrily,* "I crashed." *He rolls his sleeve up to his elbow and shows a road rash that looks like a burn with a uniform pattern of pebble imprints. »Huh?« I utter in surprise. My poor kitten, I feel bad for him. What can I do to make you feel better? Let me blow on the wound, I love you, don't go yet, please. All these thoughts are bouncing around in my head like those little balls in a pinball machine.*

Nine stages, two crashes, excellent statistics. A few words, a kiss for the little one, and then: "We have to go. We'll be late for the helicopter." *Wait. What?*

REST DAY

SEPTEMBER 2, 2019

Rest day during a race. Sounds so cool! You measure a race by its rest days – up to the first one and after the second one. By the time the first rest day comes, you've already been through a fair share or the race. For some riders getting to it is the hardest part – they need time to get into the racing rhythm. Sometimes it's easier to control everything, and the air is calmer if things are put in place in the first week with a mountainous or otherwise difficult stage. The most unpleasant thing for riders is a tough stage immediately after their rest day.

Rest days are only a part of the longest stage races, the Grand Tours. Usually, but not mandatory, they land on the second and the third Monday of the race. And how are these rest days, Primož?

❝ *Busy. Rest days are a pretty delicate matter.* **❞**

Delicate? Where the hell did he pick up that word?

❝ *In the morning, we get a timetable, which we can adjust only slightly where possible. If it says lunch is at two, you can't decide to have it at quarter past three. During the Tour, or, if I'm frank, goes for all the GTs, the rhythm is pretty much fixed. Just like on race days before the stage. Three-week races, starting in other countries, usually see an additional rest day for the transfer. Like when the Giro had to return to Italy from Jerusalem, there were three rest days instead of just two.*

Otherwise, they're all the same. Maybe you get to sleep half an hour longer if you're lucky, and the anti-doping control doesn't wake you up at six. After that comes breakfast, then training, a short session, maybe two hours long and of high intensity, at least for me. Regarding that – to each their own. What you're doing also depends on the stage that comes the next day.

Then we eat, because that is what we do during the races, we eat a lot. The afternoons are usually reserved for the media. Speaking to

*reporters, fulfilling various sponsor obligations, every once in a while
we have a press conference, and, if you're lucky, you get a visit from
your family. I like to rest. We stick a massage somewhere in there, an
osteopath, I might nag the mechanics to make some adjustments,
and then we eat again – enormous quantities of food.*

*When I was riding my first Grand Tour, the Giro 2016, I thought it would
be best to do as little as possible on my first rest day. I remember we
were in South Tyrol surrounded by apple orchards. The next day was
a disaster. It was the opposite of what I was expecting, and I barely
managed to stay in the race by the skin of my teeth.*

*The body reacts very quickly when you have a break. It's like some
kind of regeneration state kicks in, and you're left with no strength,
no sharpness the next day. Towards the end of the stage, we were
pedaling like crazy in gruppetto[39] just to beat the time limit. Dreadful!
Like I was fighting for the stage win when in reality I was fighting to
survive. A rest day is a godsend if you crashed and hurt yourself, so
your body has time to catch a breath and recover.* **"**

---

[39] We'll talk a bit more about *gruppetto* later on.

DÉJÀ VU IN THE PYRENEES

Pau, France, September 2, 2019

Déjà vu. Utterly and completely. A day before a time trial, it was exactly like that day at the Tour. We drive into Pau to exactly the same hotel as last year, with camper, just like last year, we almost get stuck on the very same speed bump, and it's just as hot as the last time! Exactly the same as before the last year's Tour time trial. OK, Lev wasn't born yet.

Last time it was the Saturday before the finish in Paris. I should've known nothing good could come from that day – as I stepped out of the camper, I slipped and landed in shit. Why, oh, why do you have to poke into such strange coincidences?

Not to mention how we drove from Andorra this year; due to an impenetrable fog, in which even birds would opt for walking, we were cutting corners following the road line on the GPS screen. Then we made a strange U-turn somewhere, possibly breaking traffic regulations, being a scaredy-cat, against my will, of course, but we managed to pull out of the traffic jam in which some of the team busses got stuck until five o'clock in the morning. The roads looked much like something from Napoleon's battles or asphalt patches giving birth, with corn fields on one side and whatever else on the other. I have never been so happy to see lights popping up when we started to descend from a random hill.

Our guys, Primož and his bunch, took off in a helicopter towards Pau. They enjoyed view over little lakes in the heart of the high Andorran mountains, but then had to return to the starting point because landing in Pau was too dangerous. Cars took off towards France only at nine in the evening.

The rest day – one of the biggest catches in professional cycling, even by name. Most people probably think that cyclists spend this day lounging in a bathrobe on the balcony, cigar in hand. Fat chance!

Much like last year, there's not a café in sight. So we have to walk along the unpaved main road, where trucks are zooming by so fast they are ruining

Selection of fried seafood in France

my hairdo; one after another by the edge of the road, we're all hot, and I'm pushing the little man in the wheelbarrow in front of me. With us is someone who is dragging his feet because cyclists are not supposed to use their legs for anything else but their bike. I'm cranky, which is a classic, Vinko is hungry, and my parents are on the tail of this funny little parade of weirdos on a highway in the coastal Pyrenees.

When we finally drag ourselves to the first café, it's closed. Oh, for fuck's sake! Well, not yet, but it will be soon. OK, we can have a drink. Fine. And if we're really hungry, we can order whatever's available. »Oui, s'il vous plaît.«

The guy brings fried mussels and fried whitebait that one particular member of our crew will surely carefully inspect and then classify in the correct fish family – biologically speaking. Who cares! Fried mussels!

"The route is OK, good, fast. We looked up which parts need no breaking. I maybe have some difficulty leaning on my elbow because of the crash,**"** *says the oddball in compression socks.*

When our little squad finally gets back to the camper, we brew a pot of coffee before setting off to a parking lot by the stadium where we would spend the night. It's not far from the time trial finish. Close to where we ate with our Swiss friends on that Saturday before Paris last year, only to find out later our train would not be leaving for Paris on Sunday because one of the stations was on fire.

Before we go, he wolfs down a whole box of Linzer cookies and leaves. I'm not too fond of this expression, but I can't fairly say he ate them because it was more like he was throwing them into a relentlessly grinding milling machine. Crunch, crunch, and a cookie was gone.

STAGE TEN

SEPTEMBER 3, 2019

JURANÇON ·······▶ PAU

36.2 KM, ITT

THE MATADOR ROGLIČ SWEEPS THE COMPETITION AND TAKES THE RED JERSEY

[…] The Slovenian cycling ace Primož Roglič justified his role of the favorite and won the individual time trial in the Tour of Spain in grand style, also taking the lead in the Vuelta general classification.

The 29-year old Roglič won the 36-kilometer time trial from Jurançon to Pau (France!) with a 25-second advantage over the New Zealander Patrick Bevin. Remi Cavagna of France came in third (+0:27). Tadej Pogačar finished eleventh (+1:29). […]

On a diverse course, Roglič was leading from start to finish. At the first intermediate timing at kilometer 11, he had a 21-second advantage over his compatriot Pogačar, who started the time trial outstandingly. At the second intermediate (kilometer 24), he was 19 seconds faster than the New Zealander Bevin, and at the finish 25. […]

Roglič became the 99th rider and the first Slovene to win a stage in every of the three toughest races. In the Giro, he won three time trials in years 2016 and 2019, and in the Tour, he won a stage in 2017, and took **the queen stage** of the 2018 edition. […] (RTV MMC 2019i)

SLO 1. ROGLIČ, PRIMOŽ (JUMBO-VISMA)	36:05:29	
ESP 2. VALVERDE, ALEJANDRO (MOVISTAR)	+1:52	
COL 3. LOPEZ MORENO, MIGUEL ANGEL (ASTANA PRO)	+2:11	

can't say much more about that day. You rarely catch someone in front of you, especially with a two-minute interval, but it happened. He performed magnificently in the discipline and in that moment. Primož set off in the green jersey he was wearing instead of Quintana. Namely, the Columbian led the general and the points classification, but he could only wear one jersey – clearly the more valuable one.

AERODYNAMICS IS ESPECIALLY IMPORTANT IN TIME TRIALS, AND IT REQUIRES SPECIAL RULES. NEXT TIME YOU'RE WATCHING A TIME TRIAL, PAY ATTENTION TO SOCKS (OR THE OVERSHOES RIDERS WEAR OVER THEIR CYCLING SHOES). THEY MAY ONLY REACH UP TO HALF THE DISTANCE BETWEEN THE KNEE AND THE ANKLE.

The queen stage doesn't get its name because of its regal cuteness. It's the name of the most difficult and the most prestigious stage in the race. Not that you get crowned, if you win, but I guess you are kind of like a king of the day. It's entirely possible that riders cross a whole mountain range that day. All joking aside, for sure, there are many mountain passes and a lot of elevation, a lot of meters for the riders to overcome.

Simply put, if they started the middle climb in stage nine in Andorran Sant Julià de Lòria at 908 meters of altitude and climbed to Coll de la Gallina at 1903 meters, their elevation gain was exactly 995 meters.

The French call this kind of stage *l'etape reine*. Many times it decides the winner of the race, and it's very interesting for spectators. People are crammed on the roadside, fused into euphoric anticipation of greeting the parade of their heroes.

The fans' burden is not a small one, and we have to keep that in mind when we spill onto mountain switchbacks, or onto flats or the last corner – anywhere on the road.

No other sport allows the fans this close to their sporting heroes. There aren't 79 rows dividing us like in a stadium at a football match in the Bundesliga, nor we're packed in the stands like when we watch ski jumping in Planica. We're not even behind the rails.

Have you figured out the second thing that makes road cycling so different from other sports? It's the biggest stadium in the world; keep in mind the Tour is seen live by around 12 million people every year. At the same time, it's the only stadium where you get in for free. There are a few exceptions, but by and large you'll never need a ticket to see a road race.

So, we don't need a ticket to see the heroics of cyclists live, but we must not forget that we can fatefully influence their careers due to this sport's freedom. When we watch a race live, we have to keep ourselves and others in mind. And we can hardly wait to visit a three-week spectacle!

For this reason, we try not to jump in front of cyclists. We don't bother them ourselves or with flags, especially not in a crowd, where everyone wants to jump on the road and where there's a considerable danger of someone knocking us down or us knocking them down.

As we stand by the road that is a part of the race, we need to predict where the cyclists will ride. Let's not forget that roads are closed to traffic on climbs, and riders will always try to find the shortest route, even if it's not the correct one according to traffic rules – so don't stand there. Even though we can't truly predict anything – attacks, crashes, the weather, etc., we should always take these things into consideration anyway.

Particular attention is required at sections where the speed is very high, for instance, on descents and intermediate sprints. Cyclists will not only buzz by with lightning speed, but they'll probably also ride on the edge of the road, grass, pavement, or wherever possible. Riders (and other vehicles in the race) are sometimes descending at over 100 km/h, and sometimes cars must overtake them even when spectators take up most of the road. Nobody wants any accidents to happen, as they could be fatal. The peloton is so fast it blows skirts up even on the flats, let alone on descents.

And even if it's so hard to resist, but nevertheless – we never push cyclists, spill water on them, or touch them in any way when they're racing. Ronaldo probably wouldn't like it either if you patted him on the back while he was preparing for a penalty kick. It's also good to pay attention to your stuff; a water bottle rolling on the road could potentially take down the entire peloton.

After spending the whole afternoon at the top of a mountain pass in the Tour under the July sun we will probably suffer a heatstroke. On some similar climb in the Giro, we could as well end up with a frostbite. It's smart to be ready for all kinds of weather surprises.

But first and foremost, let's anticipate problems and closed roads, and let's not think we'll be able to drive to a legendary climb on the day of the race – we have to be there at least a day or a night before. You can encounter a lot of random crap, like being stuck somewhere for a few days even though you didn't plan for that, or a gas station running out of gas when you need it the most, of course. And this is not even such an exception; in smaller mountain towns where the peloton spends the night, the race caravan empties it. Not really a surprise if you know that a gas tank of a team bus holds about 180 gallons of gas.

Assuming the organizer of a three week race rents more than 500 hotels that are the most race friendly in a logistical sense, we have to start looking for accommodations early, or we're screwed. Or we just stay at home.

It's not easy being a cycling fan. The biggest races demand some sacrifice. Besides not being able to take a shower for three days, you also end up seeing very little of the actual race. Probably only a few seconds when riders zoom by after you've been waiting for them the whole day.

If you want to see a few consecutive stages on a Grand Tour, I strongly recommend you think everything through very carefully. All movements before, during, and after the race are very limited. Very few spectators manage to see the start and the finish of the same Tour stage. But it's easier to avoid roadblocks with a bike. Exciting!

And even though all this sounds like a sermon (and it's not intended to be one), my last bit of advice is less dictatorial – go to the race and have as much fun as you can. Moments when thousands of us, packed like sardines, are hanging by the road for hours and hours to see the riders just for a few seconds are the best ever.

I have kind of a soft spot for helicopters due to these memories – their appearance is always a signal of the upcoming climax. You will be forever bound by the moment when you stood with so many others on some climb, cheering on every rider regardless of whether he was one of yours or not. Every single one of them will expose their true self because challenging climbs are completely sincere, and you will recognize the fight of every rider in the race. These are things that people deeply appreciate.

Let's not forget about the crazily enjoyable moments you will experience the night before and the whole day through the race, probably cursing your stiff knees from standing every so often (having a bike or a chair is a good alternative), but that just goes with the territory.

Spectators are the ones that make races glorious and magnificent. The underdogs win because of them, and the wounded rise from the ashes. I really believe the spectators can sometimes be the deciding factor in a race.

People along the road are the heart of races so don't you forget the most important thing: it's forbidden to stand stiff as a board, or like you were petrified by Medusa's gaze. Do your best like the riding warriors are doing their best. Cheer from the furthest depths of your body and proudly raise your flags as high as possible. Have fun with the Belgians and Poles and then jump to the Dutch corner. I promise you won't regret it and you'll remember that adventure forever. I don't know anybody who has gone to a race and later said: »That was really awful.«

Shall I give you an example?

Tour de France, 2018. At about two in the morning, we approach the legendary climb to the Alpe d'Huez. We'd used up all the water long ago, and I got sunburned on my bike. After the stage, we had to return to the vehicles' line as soon as possible, so we didn't have any time for lunch or dinner. The base of the climb is announcing the road is closed. I shake my head adamantly; I won't bicker with police officers and pretend I don't know French. We pass by the road sign like we didn't understand what it said. On the 5th of 21 switchbacks, the gas light comes on. Oh, this is way better than any comedy because it's not even funny. A police vehicle with lights on is coming from the opposite direction. I follow it through the rooflight. Of course, it turns around and overtakes us. Blue lights are flashing in front of us, we're still driving; straight to jail, I reckon. At the Dutch corner, disco balls are lying all over the road, I swear. Music blasting, lights flashing, the crowd dancing like at a festival. A few kilometers further, the Belgians are watering themselves with beer from a hose. The police officer takes us to a dirt road where there's some room left for campers. Crazy!!! The gas station has no gas, and the firefighters have no water left, but we're at the top!

Alpe d'Huez – celebration before the stage

THE MOMENT OF TRUTH

Pau, France, the time trial day

He will start very late, and if I have to stand in the sun, by that time my face will be red as a ripe tomato. The day is tense with anticipation, kind of like a bra that's too small for you, and you're just waiting for it to pop open because there's no way it will hold. And then, you feel immense relief when you can breathe again.

It's OK to have expectations. Is it really? Expectations are the very core of all the sadness in this world. OK, stop with that nonsense – there are also numbers. And I don't mean predictions of winners and pointing fingers at favorites that almost make me puke because Slovenians are viewed merely as fleeting flukes in the world of the best, riders who sometimes get it right by pure luck. Sometimes even Slovenians think that of other Slovenians. It hurts, and it would sting Prešeren[40] himself if he knew anything about cycling. If you don't believe in yourself, and I mean really believe, your path to success will be much harder.

We're not a traditional cycling nation, but we're not a second rate one by any means. It was on Slovenian soil they found a 5200-year old wooden wheel with an axle that is supposed to be the oldest in the world.

In any case, what I had in mind were those other numbers. Not the age of the bikes or percentages, but numbers that express power, watts per kilo, or just watts. I don't like hearing about them because I feel like he's talking about quantum physics, so every now and then, I just say »uh-huh,« occasionally replacing it with a »really?« so he doesn't suspect my mind is wandering around another planet. The rule here is, the more watts, the better. Piece of cake. I still can't explain the difference between normalized and average watts. And not because I'm stupid, but because… I just think I don't need to know it. It's pointless.

---

[40] France Prešeren (1800 – 1849), Slovenian poet and author of the text of the Slovenian national anthem.

I know how many watts mean a lot of power, and I know how many indicate there is not really much of it. I don't want to destroy that little bit of romantic streak that cycling has, and I like an intuitive way of racing, instinct, attacks that sometimes cost one's head but are chivalrous and make one seen. Once, twice, six times, eighteen times, as long as I breathe, I attack.

Primož also avoids numbers in some circumstances. He says that the heart-rate monitor constricts his chest in decisive moments and prefers riding without it. When he rides all out, giving his all, he doesn't have time to look at a little screen on his handlebars informing him of the power he is exerting on his pedals; even though many times in stage races staring at the screen turns out to be the decisive factor, as it helps you to pace yourself so you don't hit the wall. His only standard is – if you win, you rode fast and hard enough. Easy.

I have digressed a little, yet again. The catch is also in how you lean forward, you know? How aerodynamic you are. You could use Primi instead of a bar sometimes. When he leans on the handlebars of a time trial bike, his back is almost completely flat. Anyhow, let's leave these complicated things to those who know something about them.

Pau. An open square in the town center made of some kind of a cold, white stone, and dotted with fountains. It's been hot since the early morning. I buy myself a black and gold, floor-length dress and a pleated bell sleeve blouse in crêped fabric. They will always remind me of the day before the time trial.

There's a kind of a monument to all the Pyrenees winners in a green park. Lev is sleeping and isn't even a little bit interested in it, but his father is among them. There's a photo of him descending like a bullet from Aubisque, and I can just hear the commentator on the Slovenian national TV enthusiastically describing his win as one of those prominent victories of grand champions. Pau shares a great deal of cycling history with the Tour. To be one of the selected few who brought the capricious Pyrenees to their knees in the past or the present is an accomplishment no one can take away from you. Wow, what a memory!

Lev couldn't care less about his dad's win in the TDF 2018

I'm thrilled when I get a pass and a parking sticker. It means we can almost see the finish line simply sitting at our table where we sip coffee in the morning. If our mobile palace manages to squeeze through the narrow gate, that is.

We waste some time watching riders inspecting the parkour. It means two hours of leaning on the wall behind a metal barrier which marks the course. Nothing's happening, and we're there long enough for me to notice all of the potentially dangerous shit on and by the road. I start thinking about everything that can go wrong. Just enough so I can, if I say so poetically, put a few logs on my fire of anxiety so it will burn up to the moment he crosses the finish line. I see drains, high curbstones, minuscule cracks in the asphalt, the uneven surface of the line markings, the direction the tree leaves tilt in the wind, and the protruding legs of the barriers. I can't understand why these haven't been banned yet. Every time I hear the sound of disc wheels, my heart skips a beat. In time, you start recognizing the sounds. Every now and then I interrupt the staring at the steaming hot asphalt under the edge of Pyrenees just to scan the surroundings for some other problem.

We wait for a long time but still no yellow in sight. We're just about to give up when a black-yellow car appears from around the corner. Yes! It's impossible to tell who the rider in front of it is from afar, but as he comes closer - the figure on the bike is so unmistakably folded onto the handlebars that it can't be anyone else but him. He's staring at his front wheel, rumbling like a giant turtle. A fast one, of course. Even though I'm hanging over the rails with a silk Slovenian flag that I ceremoniously stole just for these kinds of moments, he doesn't even flinch. Not that I expected him to. Today he's one of the top favorites.

The rest of the day consists of waiting and discussing who would stand on the last corner and who would wait at the finish. It's windy. The wind is OK for us. In this case, it's good. Primi is heavier than the other climbers, and he can fight the wind better than lighter riders.

Sometime later, the green frog finally pushes off the ramp. We're watching him on the screen in an improvised VIP section with floor covered in something that looks like a cross between sawdust and bark. It's great because I can put the little man under an umbrella. Primož is completely focused, detached.

View from the car during a recon ride

Celebrating the win in an empty parking lot

The advantage at the first intermediate time is decent. At the second, it's considerable. At the third, it's terrifying – compared to his rivals in GC, of course. After the whole day of waiting, everything passes in a fleeting moment, full of adrenaline. »You'll catch him now,« says his sports director over the com. He caught his two minutes man. Two minutes is a lot.

I'm happy, but not ecstatic. Relieved. He's where he belongs. The stage is his and so is the jersey. Tappa e maglia, the Italians would say. I have no idea how it sounds in Spanish.

We're squeezed under the podium, we need to witness this magnificent sight for the first time. He throws to me a little plush bull in a red shirt, a mascot given to the race leader. Little Lev immediately finds its tail very appealing. We wait in the back for a quick goodbye. He's much more relaxed than he was in Andorra, but, nevertheless, a curled brow and a distinctive wrinkle between eyebrows show he's fed up. He has to attend a news conference in an inflatable press center that's traveling with the race.

"Taking it easy. I have to repeat this twelve more times; I'm taking it slow." His face doesn't move when he says that. It doesn't sound arrogant but rather kind of unbelievable and a bit funny. Doable. If I take a step back, to observe it from a distance, how is that even possible? The spot where everyone craves to be, that everyone adores and desires – there is he. My Primož.

Vehicles are slowly leaving the parking lot as we make ourselves comfortable in front of the camper. We're the only ones left. We deserve a red card for being so poorly prepared for a celebration, what a bunch of amateurs. I send Vinko to a nearby bar to buy two bottles of champagne. I won't even start about how we slept for two nights in front of a store in Andorra where there's no tax on alcohol, and no one even thought of buying a bottle or two! The table looks like something's just exploded on it. A bit of everything – a melon, potato chips, crescent rolls, chorizo, sheep milk cheese. As night fell on the Pyrenees in the background, we filled up the water tank and drove to the edge of Europe. The air was filled with a smell of the sea, and I heard waves in the distance, and probably Basque crickets. Atlantic cliffs and red peppers, bonjour.

STAGE ELEVEN

SEPTEMBER 4, 2019

SAINT-PALAIS ·······▸ URDAX-DANTXARINEA

180 KM, HILLY

BASQUE ITURRIA WINS THE FIRST STAGE IN HIS CAREER AFTER A FANTASTIC ESCAPE

[…] A day after the individual time trial in Pau, the Tour of Spain favorites took a bit of rest before Friday's grueling mountain stage. Mikel Iturria was the strongest in the breakaway, which managed to gain an 18-minute advantage. Primož Roglič kept the red jersey. The first attempts to escape started soon after the start. A breakaway group of 14 riders formed and gained seven minutes on the peloton after 30 kilometers. […]

There were 14 riders in the day's breakaway, and Iturria attacked heroically 25 kilometers from the finish. Even though the rest of the riders tried to chase him, he managed to hold on and celebrated his first professional win. […]

Roglič and his Team Jumbo-Visma didn't need to concern themselves with the breakaway's success, as there were no riders who could endanger his lead in the GC. The Slovenian crossed the finish line in 19th place. The rest of the Slovenians crossed the finish line within the time of the peloton. […]
(RTV MMC 2019j)

```
SLO 1. ROGLIČ, PRIMOŽ (JUMBO-VISMA)            41:00:48
ESP 2. VALVERDE, ALEJANDRO (MOVISTAR)           +1:52
COL 3. LOPEZ MORENO, MIGUEL ANGEL (ASTANA PRO)  +2:11
```

When a large group of riders crosses the finish line together, i.e., the peloton or the bunch, the same time is attributed to everyone. That's why it is quite common, especially in stages that finish with a sprint, for all riders to have the same finishing time. The winner is attributed the time he needed to complete the stage while all the others who finished in a group, regardless whether in 11th or 28th place, have »s. t.« written next to their names – same time. Sometimes they all have the same time. The French slap an m. t. next to their names instead of s. t. – *même temps*. And occasionally we'll see an @ or simply winner's time.

But, carefully, there is something called the three-second rule. It's been in use since 2017 for flat stages to ensure better safety in stressful finishes. It might be a little confusing, but we'll just let it stay that way because even riders (you can guess which one I have in mind) don't know exactly when it applies and when not. It can be used in all stage races. In the Tour roadbook, the three-second rule is strictly defined.

So what does it mean? Not everyone has to cross the finish line tightly together, but there cannot be more than 2.99 seconds of a gap at the most for the winner's time to count for them.

Let's say a sprinter wins. Instead of a typical bunch, some scattered cyclists follow. As long there isn't a time gap greater than 3 seconds between the rear wheel of one cyclist and the front wheel of the next one, then they are still considered to be crossing the finish line in the same time; 3 seconds at a speed of 60 km/h translate to 50 meters!

PEPPERS AND CLIFFS

Saint-Jean-de-Luz, France, September 4, 2019

Another unsettled bill from last year. Basque Country, fragrant with mint. French Basque Country this time, just like then. Maybe Pau broke the spell? We couldn't find a flat surface to park during the night, so the rear of the camper is hanging towards the beach, and I feel like a bat. When even those few surfers vans that were parked beside us during the night vanish in the morning, it soon becomes clear that we shouldn't be here. There's lush greenery all around us, and the sea is roaring. The air is thick with humidity, the beach is wide, open, full of sand and rocks, and it's windy, very windy, of course.

We were planning to stay here on the Atlantic coast until Saturday and then return home. The little one and I could then stay with our friends, Špela and Primož, who joined me with the idea of making it together to Madrid.

But then it dawns on us that there is pretty much no sense in lying around the beach when we have the red jersey, and the stage finish is not far away. We have all day, the start is late, and our sticker opens barricades when the road is closed off for the rest of the world. Ha! This privilege is a first for me. When I come to the beach for the second time, the sea has retreated almost ten meters. At the end of the beach, on a crumbling rock guarding the edge of the water, there's a small house, white with blue shutters – this isn't France, it's the Basque Country. It's crumbling a bit, but mainly it's overgrown with strong, waxy greenery. I like it here; Basque Country has always been good to us. Except last year in the Tour. But I have already forgiven it for that. Bloody mint and Espelette pepper.

We're driving along narrow roads, typical for this part of the world. Steep and tight turns, the most beautiful patches of green grass, the most precarious bridges that make me step out every time to look whether we'll be able to drive across, and the typical white houses with wooden beams on the facades and dried peppers, hanging from ropes.

Nothing happens. We park on soft grass just before the breakaway reaches the last climb. The narrow gap between an iron fence and a wall, overgrown with moss, is too tight for the stroller. I make it to the stage exactly at the moment Primož is descending from it, and I push through to the fence when he's about to be dragged off to the anti-doping control. A few words, »hi, hi,« he gives me a stuffed bear, dressed in green, which later turns out to be a lynx with a helmet. I admit I secretly shed a tear when they announce the lider de la clasificacion general, *and my guy appears through the door; my guy, the one that the cycling world is fascinated with, and they are not holding back to show him.*

Our search for an open restaurant on our way back was futile. We'll sleep in a camp tonight, not in the wild. The only plot we can find doesn't have a million-dollar view, but it's cool because there are showers, toilets, and a washing machine. It was raining the whole night through. In the morning, we wake up to a shitty weather, dark clouds about us, spewing tiny droplets, and an angry ocean below us.

STAGE TWELVE

SEPTEMBER 5, 2019

CIRCUITO DE NAVARRA ········▶ BILBAO

171 KM, HILLY

GILBERT WINS, ROGLIČ AND POGAČAR CONCLUDED A SUCCESSFUL DAY WITH A FIST BUMP [...]

Philippe Gilbert is the winner of stage 12 of the Tour of Spain. [...] Primož Roglič easily sustained the general classification lead.

Gilbert was one of the riders in the breakaway. The experienced rider, whose main goal for this season is the upcoming World Championship (he won the rainbow jersey in 2012), wisely chose the right moment to attack. Spaniards Alex Aranburu and Fernando Barcelo were the only ones able to follow the Belgian, but the 19-second advantage Gilbert managed to grab was enough for the descent and the finish on the streets of Bilbao. [...]

The group of favorites crossed the finish line just over three minutes behind the winner. The red jersey, worn by Primož Roglič for the second consecutive day, wasn't targeted. In the final kilometers of the stage, on the streets of the largest city in the Basque Country, the Slovenian aces Roglič (Jumbo-Visma) and Tadej Pogačar (UAE) were seen smiling and chatting. Just before the finish line, they bumped fists to mark a successful day. [...] (RTV MMC 2019k)

SLO 1. ROGLIČ, PRIMOŽ (JUMBO-VISMA)   44:52:08

ESP 2. VALVERDE, ALEJANDRO (MOVISTAR)   +1:52

COL 3. LOPEZ MORENO, MIGUEL ANGEL (ASTANA PRO)   +2:11

Aday in the red jersey. How does it feel when you're leading the general classification in the three-week race?

❝ *Until you get dressed before the start, nothing is different. Well, your jersey is of a different color. But the day itself is just like any other. You wake up, and you feel like you've been hit by a train. I try to follow my usual morning routine as much as I can. We get a schedule the night before, and it contains information about what time breakfast is and when they are going to collect our baggage[41], at what time we are to leave for the start, the approximate duration of the transfer to the start and from the finish to a new hotel and such so we can get our heads around it.*

We pack a bag of stuff that we'll need, or things we'd like to have handy after the stage; a handbag, so to speak – phones, earphones, a change of clothes, etc. When the bus arrives at the start, we change into racing gear, pin on our numbers, and change the lenses on our racing glasses, if necessary. The toilet is definitely a point of interest before the stage, ha. Then we, riders, have a meeting with our sports directors. They usually make a short introduction to the stage, even though we research them ourselves before. We go through the plan, dangerous sections of the course, and discuss what we have to pay special attention to. We drink a coffee or two and eat a snack. Then we go to sign in. The zone with team busses is usually open, so there's a lot of people there. If you have time, you give out some autographs, do some photos, but sometimes you just can't. You have to be careful in the crowd, so you don't have a stupid accident. Someone can take you down unintentionally, or you can knock someone over, again, unintentionally. In the last week of the Vuelta, I had two policemen accompanying me from the bus to the signing platform.

---

[41] Due to the daily dynamic and different start and finish locations, the cycling caravan moves every day. Riders rarely stay at one place and in the same hotel for more than one night, so special traveling logistics come into play. Every day they prepare the luggage at the designated time and soigneurs make sure it finds its way to the bus storage compartment before the bus departs.

The race leader is always treated a bit differently on the stage. The presenter pays him the most attention, asks couple of questions, so it can take a while. There could be some larger TV crew present as well, that would like to get your statement. Then there's also a so-called village, where riders can grab a bite or have a drink. I don't hang around there much. If I have the opportunity and time, I go back to the bus.

Then we go to the start line. There's no rule about where you have to stand. The team doesn't have to stick together, and your racing number isn't important. It's more or less about taking a photograph, so better-known riders stand in front. With the red jersey, you're in front, of course. A small town that paid to host a stage start can boast with a photo from the start for years. We take off exactly at the designated time, but that's not a real start yet. The actual start is at kilometer zero. There's nothing different for the red jersey during the race. Well, you have the right to ride at the front of the group, you and your team. But you have to earn that position in any case. If I wear the leader's jersey, I don't take my feed bag myself, but that depends on the team's internal agreement anyway, so it can be arranged either way with or without the leader's jersey.

The most noticeable difference comes after the finish line. If the stage finishes with a full-gas sprint, I go to cool down on the rollers[42]. If you have to sprint uphill to the finish line, it's not good to completely stop with a pulse of 200 bpm. After that, everyone except the jerseys' holders and the stage winner return to their busses. If you wear one of the jerseys you still have some tasks left. First, you must give a short statement to journalists or television reporters. But even that comes after the soigneur helped you to look presentable again, you cooled down, had a drink, some water, basically a quick recovery, and then you go to the podium. When the ceremony's over, the anti-doping test

---

[42] Rollers and trainers are two different things, but the main point is you put your bike on a trainer and you can spin the pedals as if you were on a static bike.

Keeping the red jersey busy in the finish area

awaits. Every race has a mobile office, a trailer, or a special mobile home where a doctor does the test. If you're the race leader, you go for a test after every stage. The same goes for the stage winner in all of the WT races. I wore the leader's jersey for more than 30 days last year, which means at least that many tests, plus tests at home, at the training camp, in races, etc. But that's the way it should be.

After the anti-doping control, there are more TV, radio, and organizer statements, and only then a press conference in the press center. There's a lot of media work. Hop into the car, and off we go. I try to eat something during the drive and rest a little, but we all know what sleeping in a car looks like. The drive to the hotel is not long if you're lucky, but usually you're not. I'm the last to come to the hotel; others arrive there by bus much earlier. I do pretty much the same things at the hotel as the others – a massage, maybe an osteopath, dinner, try to sleep. All of that comes into play very late if you know that stages end at about five or six in the afternoon. And it's really difficult to fall asleep with a full stomach after a late dinner. **"**

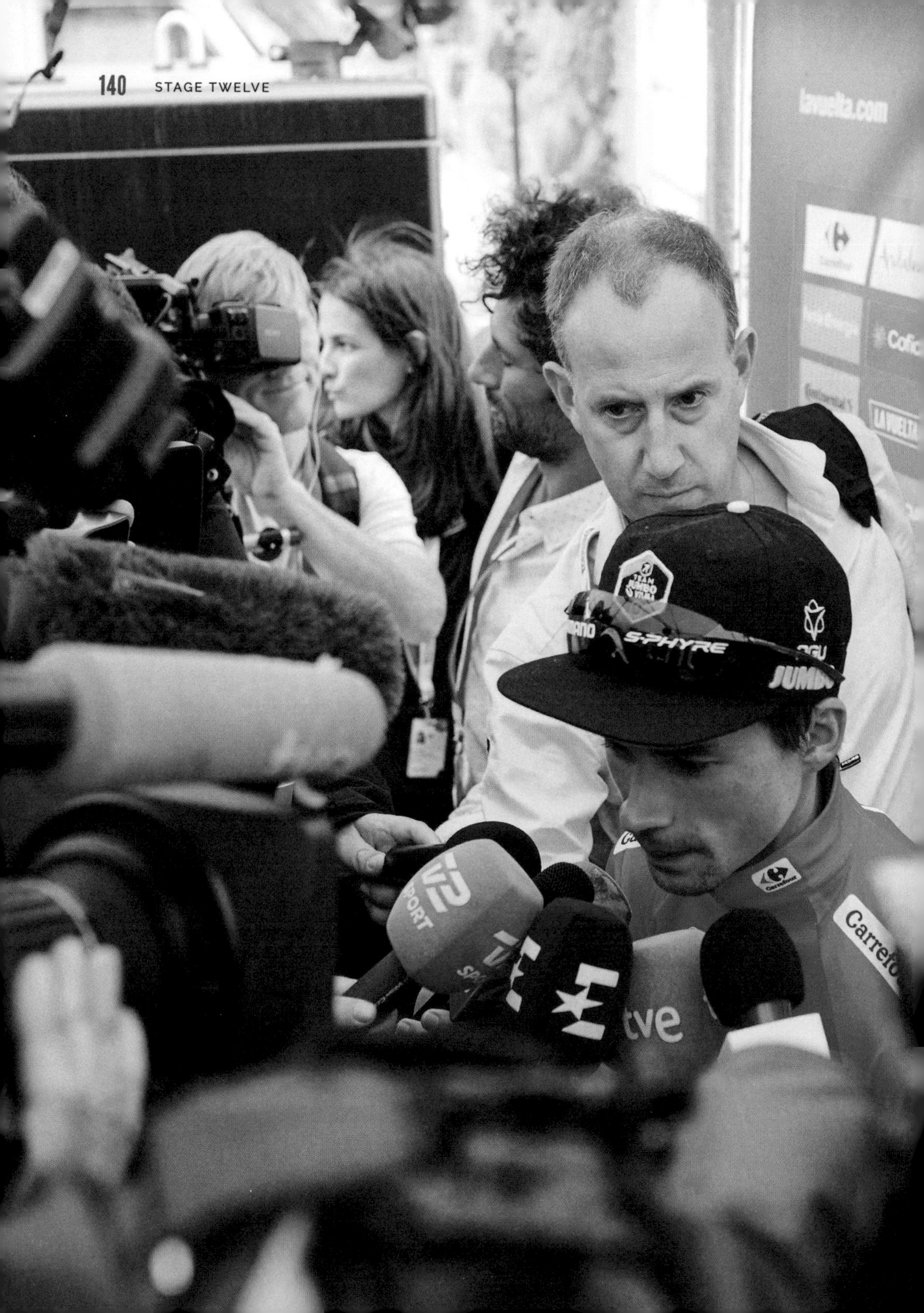
lavuelta.com
LA VUELTA
S-PHYRE
JUMBO
Carrefour
tve
SPORT

CALM BEFORE THE STORM

Saint-Jean-de-Luz, France, September 5, 2019

The next morning is much like the night, miserable and covered with heavy sky, with waves crashing over the rocks below and foaming to the beach. To reach it, there's an endless spiral of stairs coiling among low bushes and an occasional cactus. I don't feel like going to the beach. But the fragrance stays in my memory. The scent of summer passed by too quickly, of sweet rain, slightly salted from mist rising above the ocean; the air that wants to be warm and scatter the clouds smells of something green that reminds me of the Croatian island of Pag, but I can't put my finger on exactly what. When I take a deep breath, it's thick, salty, and humid. It's raining. What now?

We quickly come to the agreement that it's best to go to Bilbao. After an unsuccessful pit stop in San Sebastian, where we just couldn't find any space in the old part of town, we only stop at the side of the road, so my family runs around the corner to a pier with a view of the city.

We came here every year after the Tour. I'm delighted with the beautiful memories. I explain to my folks where the classic of San Sebastián ends and how scared I was when, in quite similar weather, we made a low flight over the famous Santa Clara Island, thickly overgrown with the Basque forest. I remember a building on it, but I have no idea what it was. We flew in a tin, well, in a minute plane for five people that miraculously made it from Antwerp in Belgium. We once ate txuleta, beef with little fried green peppers typical of Basque Country, in the old town. And a year earlier, we dulled our pain with a six-pack of beer at the La Concha beach, going on and on until it ends at the stump under the rampart that hides the old town center.

It was the night after the race (we used the cans as cold compresses on the sore body parts before emptying them), the one where everyone was anxiously staring at Jaizkibel, the mysterious climb that was to give the new winner of the old prestigious race. As it happened, a fairly open and wide road, framed by trees, swiped a fair share of riders in a mass crash, and Primož found himself in that pile of bodies and bikes.

I was frantically calling home - when you're there, at the scene, you know nothing – remote knowledge is typically necessary for the road races. He got up, they said. And then I stood on a trashcan, fortunately leaning on a streetlight, to see over a bunch of Basque heads whether he really got back on the bike.

I can't believe »he got up« satisfied me. He made it to the finish line, eventually, light years after the peloton, but he did. And there was one lap left to the end of the race. I jumped off the trashcan, almost breaking both of my ankles in worn-out sandals, and pushed my way to the fence. I

San Sebastian

showered the policeman by the road with questions, but he was indifferent and didn't answer any. Then a boy that miraculously spoke English told me that Roglič sat into an ambulancia. *Shit. Shit. That doesn't happen often. I completely forget about the race, find his team's hotel in the roadbook, and almost run to it.*

No one answers the phone, and no one knows anything, so I sit in the lobby until he arrives. The sun has almost gone down. They thought he broke his hip. Luckily he only sustained a blow that hard, he couldn't pedal anymore. I fell in love with the Basque fortress with a backdrop instantly. The clasica ciclista *remains to be conquered some other time.*

When we leave San Sebastián behind in the present, Bilbao emerges soon after Santander. The sun shows up when the race is climbing the slopes in the second half of the stage. As much as I can see of it through the rear window of the camper, I like it. High, cold storefronts of expensive shops paint a picture of an old, neatly groomed lady. It reminds me of Palma de Mallorca. The town is beautiful and clean and gives off a vibe of wealth. We find a top parking spot beside a large park – we're almost a part of the caravan now. The break will obviously succeed. Lev blows a gasket so much that all four of us together can't calm him down, and that's the most dramatic event of the day. My little, sweet, soft love that sometimes makes me wonder what to do with it.

Philippe Gilbert attacks from the break on the last climb, much like those in the classics. If you were to connect the dots after the battle, you might say his attack was to be expected. I push my way through the barriers in Vinko and Mattia's company to the road a few meters behind the finish line, where soigneurs stand. Primož doesn't know we're here. He only notices us from the podium. I admit, his reaction is cute.

After the road transforms into an almost deserted battlefield, and they are already stacking the fencing on the trucks that will depart immediately towards the finish of tomorrow's stage, we're still waiting on the gentleman in the red jersey who is in a tent, giving statements into microphones, weaved around his head like a wreath. Those who couldn't get to him earlier intercept him at the fence, and a journalist who obscures my view asks him how come he's finally smiling today. The Spanish media deemed him an ice king concerning journalists. He replies he's smiling because he sees me behind them. They'll probably say now that not only is he cold, he's also flippant. I get two minutes of his time and goodbye.

We continue our journey along the coast. We stop at a wide sandy beach in Laredo, take the grill out, and set it up on the sidewalk. These are all the perks of camping life. Rain starts to sprinkle, gentle rain. Drops falling on the canopy are creating some kind of music, and the darkness is not pitch black yet, thus allowing me to go far towards the sea, where my shoes sink into the wet sand completely. Tomorrow, tomorrow, real hell will break loose.

STAGE THIRTEEN

SEPTEMBER 6, 2019

BILBAO ·······▶ LOS MACHUCOS. MONUMENTO VACA PASIEGA

166 KM, MOUNTAIN

POGAČAR AND ROGLIČ FRIED THE FAVORITES IN THE INFERNO OF LOS MACHUCOS

Slovenia is the new Columbia. Stage 13 of the Vuelta 2019 brought an unforgettable day for Slovenian cycling. At the top of the Los Machucos climb, Tadej Pogačar celebrated a victory while Primož Roglič fortified his red lead with second place.

Slovenians have never been so dominant in the history of Grand Tours as today. A look at the general classification is compelling. The leader Roglič has an advantage of 2:25 in front of Valverde, Pogačar is third (+3:01). Nairo Quintana was the first of the favorites to attack at the Los Machucos climb, a hellishly steep, narrow road (gradients rose to 25%), but Roglič and Pogačar maintained their pace through the crowd of excited fans and then unanimously launched a deadly attack that saw Quintana, Lopez, and finally Valverde being thrown out of the game. [...]

With three kilometers to go, Roglič and Pogačar attacked in unison. Only Valverde was able to follow in the first few meters, but even he soon started to struggle, while the Slovenians had remarkably strong legs on the slope that forced many riders to zigzag while trying to maintain their balance.

With a few hundred meters of flat to the finish line, Roglič gentlemanly left the stage win to Pogačar, who took his second stage win in his first three-week race. [...] (RTV MMC 20191)

SLO	1. ROGLIČ, PRIMOŽ (JUMBO-VISMA)	49:20:28	
ESP	2. VALVERDE, ALEJANDRO (MOVISTAR)	+2:25	
SLO	3. POGAČAR, TADEJ (UAE TEAM EMIRATES)	+3:01	

Did we witness the Slovenian alliance that put the world cycling elite on its knees? Maybe they had an advantage in communication. Slovenian is still a language of mystery in the international cauldron. So let's clear this up. They didn't go together as friends, which they undoubtedly are, but because they determined that they could help each other. Together, but each for himself, they fought the others. They both had to gain something from this opportune collaboration.

We often see riders of different teams collaborating in races. It's a kind of a pact among riders, often with a win-win outcome; those who participate recognize a benefit in it. The Slovenian pair showed exactly that in stage 13, a perfect collaboration. Besides, they were both in a league of their own compared to their rivals. We saw one of the most magnificent moments in Slovenian cycling.

I won't get into geometry, but what you see here, is the profile of the final climb of stage 13. The horizontal axis shows kilometers, the vertical altitude and the numbers on the slope show gradients of the climb. Zero stands for a pure flat, while a minus, logically, shows the road descending. Stage profiles usually also indicate the average gradient of the respective road that leads up a mountain.

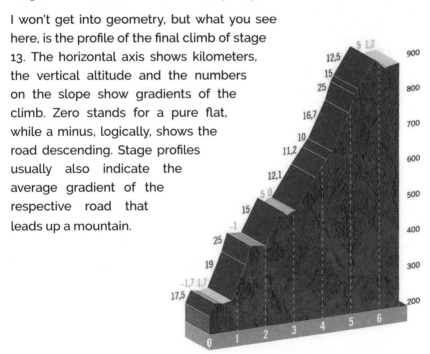

RAMPAS INHUMANAS

Laredo, Cantabria, Spain, September 6, 2019

Rain, again. I regret the first day I cut off my jeans' legs because it was the only hot day up until now. Which means I only wore them once. Great move. I stroll to the beach under the yellow-black team umbrella I pinched at the Giro. I put on sandals over my socks. I'll regret that soon, too.

The small dunes, starting just as you step off a paved path, are almost like little »hills«. The trail, marked with a low picket fence, is obscured by sand that wind blew in in the days before. I can see from afar the beach has been plowed. It was not as much plowed as groomed with huge ruts that later turned out to be from a digger taking away seaweed that the sea brought in during the night.

Among the dunes, something like a pampas grass grows. This is how I would imagine the Irish coast if I knew what it looked like. Wide, full of grasses that remind you of Copenhagen and a bit of Rio de Janeiro, with a majestic rock formation by the side, and Mallorca just before you reach the airport. The rain is getting more relentless by the minute, loudly beating against my umbrella. My socks get soaked immediately, and no one knows where Vinko is. He's probably dissected the beach up and down and from left to right. His blood type must be seawater.

I'm glancing at the sky as usual, looking for signs among the clouds that would convince me the weather was going to dry up in the race's decisive moments. I can't imagine the poor guys falling on their scrawny bottoms when their bikes get flipped over their rear wheels on a wet, 31% climb, not even in the best of comedies. And this wouldn't be one – it would be a drama.

Anyway, because we want to go up the Machucos, an infernal climb, we must leave Cantabria for Asturias. I remember the mighty chestnuts lining the road. It takes us through a narrow valley scattered with stony haciendas, much like the ones you see in Mexican telenovelas. Round water wells blurrily emerge through heavy wrought iron fences, rounding the image of luxurious yards lined with colorful bushes – why have only one if you can have three. It feels like we went back at least 200 years. Surrounding peaks, some of them rounded softly at the top and covered with inviting green grass, are precipitous, and courageous spruce hang off steep slopes here and there.

We finally find ourselves at a crossroads. The road crawls right in the shape of a Y with arrows pointing out the race's direction. I always wonder how the hell the whole peloton, flying by at least 60 km/h with blurred vision because they are barely alive at this point, will notice that little piece of fluorescent cardboard stuck to a post. They just can't, no way. Which must mean they just follow the others in the conglomerate, which keeps shifting shape like a school of sardines. We turn left.

A policeman stops us. I push forward from the rear of the camper, asking him about the road further up. »Pericolosa, con este machina« – dangerous with this tractor-trailer; will we survive? We'll climb Los Machucos from the other side.

»Si, si,« nods the bearded man with a red paddle in his hand. The road is narrow but not dangerous. I'm kind of relieved, but then again, if on the other side we have rampas inhumas, then what are the chances of this side being stomped into nice alpine switchbacks? But if the authorities here say it's doable, it must be true. A stone bridge, an overture into the road waiting behind the corner, is narrow and mysterious like a time portal, a doorway to a place far away. It doesn't take me long to realize how correct this thinking is and how we should have taken the stony narrowness as a sign telling us not to push forward.

Our inevitable end begins very quickly with a concrete road leading into a corner squeezed among a few houses. The sun must reach this edge very rarely and of course, the road is still wet. Despite the brave words of confidence, the tires start to burn on the killer incline, and the camper starts slipping backward. »Bloody hell, mother of god, please stop; I don't want to die this way!«

General panic kicks in, and I can only think about where to put the little guy so at least he survives, and how many houses we'll knock down in this pitiful neck of the woods that should be a glorious road. Suddenly, the camper stops. A terrible smell fills the air. We're stuck in the middle of the road, precariously leaning back.

My heart is pounding, and I'm looking at the others in fear because it seems like nobody knows what just happened. We can't go back because we're slipping too much. We don't know if we're able to move forward. A risky move turns out to be a good one, and after a few meters, we stop by the side of the road.

If we have to stay here until Madrid, it's fine with me. Just as long as this shitstorm is over. To the right of the small road, there's a cemetery on a high terrace carved into the slope. Would they bury me here if the camper didn't stop? Oh, stop it, you idiot.

When we calm down after this adrenaline stunt, I realize something else that's slightly more painful – I won't be able to see the race. Why, pretty please, you bunch of morons, with all the vast mountain ranges at your disposal, stuff the race up some forgotten fucking hill you can only climb with a pickax and is as accessible as Mount Everest in flip-flops? You're giving me a heart attack before the race even begins! Not to mention my phone died.

»Lora, it's because this is the hill everyone's been talking about for the last three months. Everyone is waiting for the clutches to burn on inhumane inclines with a 31 percent gradient. Rampas inhumanas. Can you imagine it? It's steeper than Innsbruck. So what, if people don't get up there. The whole world will be watching!« Smartass biologist Vinko, stick to your fish. Innsbruck was one of the worst things I've ever seen. You only realize how steep it is when you turn around and look down, when your ankles get stretched into a gymnastic element your joints didn't know was possible. Oh, and get this – walking up doesn't compare to riding up on a bike. You can be ready and aware it's hard. But until you try and ride it, all the contemplating and talk is just a bunch of baloney.

I decide the bearded cop was a) drunk, b) has sent us here intentionally, like be my guests, you stupid tourists, or c) he didn't give a rat's ass.

I should go back down there and smack him on the kisser. What's wrong with you, hombre?

No, no, no, I have to find a solution. I sit on a low wall by the cemetery high above the road and observe hordes of people going by on foot or bikes, with backpacks, chairs, and flags.

They're not going for a walk with a flag, are they?! So it can't be that far? I call Mattia. I will be the end of this guy. He doesn't know; no one knows anything. Hours go by. Vinko takes the mountain bike to check the road ahead. I walk. The slope is dreadful. We're really lucky the camper stopped. If we had gone any further, it might have broken in two. It would have been even worse.

I'm not talking, just mulling things over in my head. I pour red wine into a plastic cup, take a piece of sheep cheese, and break off a bit of baguette.

Every once in a while, someone takes a photo in front of the camper. There's a red plush bull that the red jersey gets on the podium sitting on the dashboard. And every now and then, I hear someone say familia de Primo(z), familia del lider.

Of course, there is no TV signal. Vinko comes back. He was at the top. It's at least eight kilometers. Shit. Kill yourself, Lora. What should I do? What? Should I put the little man into my backpack and ride my bike up there?

I'll walk. I'll put him into a carrier and carry him to the top. If all these people can do it, you'll manage, too. I fill my backpack, take my pass, the dead phone, the kid in the carrier, and my mother, and let's go.

We soon need to stop for a rest, basically just above where we stopped and stare down. A little white car stops at our camper. If he says we have to move, I'll kick his ass. Where could we go, smartass? Talk to the schmuck that sent us up here. I'm livid to the point of foaming at the mouth. Just as we press on, I think I hear my name.

Someone at the camper is waving at me. I finally realize it's the petite gentleman from Switzerland, Mattia. If he thinks I'm going back down there so he can tell me I can't go to the top, he's sorely mistaken. We scream at one another for a while. At last, mother, the little guy without a voting right, and I decide to go back down. Due to the sense or no sense of going further, I'm given the final authority. The agent, who is practically almost a part of our family, says not to panic. Right. He drives someone somewhere and returns. We'll drive up with the little white car.

Good god! Time stands still. He comes back with the general manager of one of the teams in the shotgun seat while the three of us scramble into the back seat and the chassis almost drags against the pavement from the load. I won't even go into the state of the road. Coming out of a short wooded area, it continues hanging on the left bank of a narrow V-shaped valley. There's asphalt missing in some parts, and it's bulging in others so much that we almost get stuck. The gradients match what one would expect from the other side of the rampas inhumanas. *We catch up with our fisherman, riding his bike up there for the second time, and a bit further, my dad, also on his bike. And then we stop.*

They're not letting people through anymore because there's no room at the top. We have to move to the left, to some kind of a goat trail, which they call road that is also ludicrously steep. I don't trust the handbrake to keep the car in place while those two in front prepare to argue with the gentleman directing the traffic. A smell I subconsciously connect to road races is the smell of a burnt clutch. And of burnt tires, while we're at it. However, I must admit I probably can't distinguish one from another.

God knows what's happening in the race now. I sadly look at the team cars driving by; they'll replace the busses in the finish zone. Most of the riders will have to put on their windbreakers after the stage and return down the same way they came up. Our two »cyclists« ride by for the second time while Mattia and that other manager speak in four languages on their phones, while also talking to the guy directing the traffic, showing him the logos of the manager's team clothing and all the accreditations we have. It pays off in the end. There's really not much room at the top.

But the drama is not over yet. At the top, the security guy doesn't let me into the tent because I don't have the right accreditation.

I'm holding a two-and-a-half-month-old who's watching curiously out of his snug blanket, a thick fog surrounds us, and humidity is making my hair stick to my face. I don't have the energy for another fight, so I'll spend my day stuck behind a rock wall, scattered with cow shit, and hope the little guy doesn't get pneumonia. For now, I'm just leaning against the wall, hurt

At the top of Los Machucos

and on the verge of tears. Not because I'm not in the tent, but because Fernando over there doesn't have one iota of humanity within him.

I'll survive; I'm breathing even though I'm sad. Life is not a piece of cake. The wind is blowing, and it's very cold. I'm hugging the little one close while trying to explain that everything will be fine – these things happen sometimes. Lev is giving me a bewildered look, but he's calm. Maybe because he's cold. After a while, they almost have to beg me to go inside, but I don't have a choice if I don't want my kid to freeze to death. I'm thinking about stepping on the security guy's foot with all of my magnificent weight as I pass by.

All those hours of injustice I suffered today quickly disappear, and the riders are suddenly at the foot of the climb. They're just about to ride up. What the whole cycling world had been anticipating for months and months will be resolved in 30 minutes, or maybe a few more. When the breakaway riders start the climb, they already have some advantage. The head of the bunch is mostly yellow but soon turns into the light blue of Astana trying to get their captain into the best position possible. Riding a climb of this kind, you have to be in front. If the road is wide, those battling for the top spots in the GC don't need to start in front because they have enough time to make it to the front. In this instance, they don't, as the road is narrow.

The bunch is getting thinner and thinner, and the decimated peloton turns into a handful of lean, emotionless grimpeurs waiting for the first sword to be drawn. I think to myself how the only sound to be heard in the group rolling over the concrete goat path is heavy breathing – like in a herd of asthmatic elephants. I spot the red jersey and the famous turning of hips. He's holding on, but I can't figure out if he's just acting or he's really OK.

The steep slope conjures a recollection to the last decisive ramp in the Grand Tour. Passo di Mortirolo in the Italian Alps during this year's Giro in May. Not Mortirolo, please, anything but Mortirolo! I hold my fist to my mouth, and suddenly I become insecure like a hand-built shack in hurricane winds. Damn you, head! Where did you find the fucking Mortirolo now?

The tail of the peloton climbing the rampas inhumanas

It's a painful memory, I admit. Someone once said about Mortirolo that it's so difficult, he would cry at the top had he any strength left. Dreadfully painful and with horrible weather coming in as the night fell over the Tour of Italy in the middle of the day, bringing cold, fog, icy rain, and wind. The apocalyptic raging of the elements only emphasized the threatening background while I watched Primož fading with my heart bleeding. He was as pale as a ghost, his eyes lifeless, with pupils hanging over the corneas, saliva mixed with icy Alpine rain hanging from his chin almost to the handlebars, and the last strand of snot, everything dripping away along with the dreams he had for that day.

I never understood that saliva, disgustingly oozing from the face, almost to the point of turning into a foam. Even if I think of Bjørndalen, the famous Norwegian biathlete, always somehow reaching the finish in that state – I never liked to watch him win. But after a while and a lot of my own kilometers later, it became crystal clear; the foam is there because you have no strength left to spit.

He found himself alone, floating somewhere among the leaders, abandoning, fighting for life, to be or not to be, and the peloton, dragging himself towards the top on a vertical road through dark green woods. I kept pacing between the TV and the bed, pushing my head into the pillow, inventing a mix of sniffling, shaking, and screaming, praying for it to end. I was stroking the ball of life in my lap, crying, and telling myself I couldn't let myself sink into a nervous breakdown because I'd end up giving birth. After a while, a long while, I'm sure, I went back to the TV and realized only 200 meters had passed.

Deadly silence ruled the living room, only to be harshly cut by our voices cheering him on; us, as wounded as he is, staring at the screen, compassionately, motionless. Somewhere between crying and swearing, it became obvious to me – he was finished, he bonked big time. Besides a bunch of questions about the point of his racing torturing my mind, I can only think of how someone should help him, for god's sakes, and why is he doing this, and please, pretty please, let it stop once and for all because I just can't cope anymore, I can't! Someone stop this crucifixion in front of the whole world, stop it! When he crawls to the top defiantly, his lips are blue. Because of the lack of oxygen or because he's freezing? I have no idea, but I'm thinking he shouldn't take the windbreaker because I don't know if he's capable of letting the handlebars go and staying on the bike. On the other hand, he should take it to avoid coming from the descent like an ice cube.

And here's another one of my demons, the descent. This one is technical and challenging, closed, and with a lot of turns. It's wet, and the riders are freezing – the highest measured speed that day was 83 km/h. Thank god I didn't watch it. They didn't need to tell me who was the fastest descending.

It's hard to admit sometimes that this is just the way it is with cycling. It's hard to accept sometimes that someone does this of his own free will and that all the suffering and the state of not knowing whether you'll drop dead or manage to push to the top is completely normal. And yet, the peloton walks on the edge of existence every day. They ride on the brink of consciousness, sometimes holding the handlebars with only one hand, catching a breath where terrain permits and the gradient eases up a bit, and then they push forward. All the way to the purple lips, bloodless faces, and fire in their lungs.

No! I decide Mortirolo will not happen again on this possibly most decisive climb of the Tour of Spain. Under the tarp where the stage is being broadcasted live, Pogačar gains a few meters on the chase. The terrain is illusive, and it's hard to read how much, when, and who. It's OK, stay calm. There's a cyclist in front of the favorites' group, a Frenchman. When the camera returns to Pogačar, he has a red shadow. Yes! Slowly but surely, they're slipping away from the others. Slovenia is at the top of the world. Just shy of the flamme rouge, indicating there's one kilometer to the finish line, they catch the Frenchman. It doesn't matter what happens now. They destroyed them. They gave them a lecture about riding steep climbs. The most difficult in the category. Everything's great, I'm relieved.

Before they ride through the last corner, I start to move to the finish line. I can't see the road anyway. I know he won't win, but it's been a beautiful day, completely not Italian. Thank you. Thank you. He waves from the podium, and he's one of those descending on the other side of Machucos by car. They drive past us, and the car stops by our camper for a second so I can get a kiss through the window. Now we only have to drag the stuck beast back to flat terrain, and then we're done.

STAGE FOURTEEN

SEPTEMBER 7, 2019

SAN VICENTE DE LA BARQUERA ·······➤ OVIEDO

188 KM, FLAT

BENNET WINS THE SPRINT, MEZGEC SUFFERS AN ILIUM FRACTURE

Pibernik spent the better part of the stage in the breakaway that was caught
four kilometers before the finish.

Sam Bennett won stage 14 of the Tour of Spain with a decisive sprint a kilometer
before the finish that saw a massive crash. Primož Roglič managed to avoid the
fall, but Luka Mezgec was considerably worse off.

MEZGEC TOOK THE BRUNT OF IT

The course climbed slightly in the last kilometer, and at that point, a number
of riders crashed, the world champion Alejandro Valverde and Slovenians Luka
Mezgec and Tadej Pogačar among them. Mezgec sustained the worst injuries and was
immediately taken to an ambulance. […] The GC leader Primož Roglič had to stop,
but luckily he didn't fall. Due to the crash happening in the last kilometer,
the peloton's lag was nullified. […] (RTV MMC 2019m)

SLO	1. ROGLIČ, PRIMOŽ (JUMBO-VISMA)	53:49:19
ESP	2. VALVERDE, ALEJANDRO (MOVISTAR)	+2:25
SLO	3. POGAČAR, TADEJ (UAE TEAM EMIRATES)	+3:01

There's a special rule that's supposed to reduce danger for the riders in the finishing kilometers of the stage. The three-kilometer rule states that, in the event of a flat tire, crash, or a mechanical failure in the last three kilometers of a stage, riders who are delayed due to one of these reasons get attributed the finishing time of those they were riding with before the incident. In this case, a whole group of riders was involved, and everyone who crashed or was stuck was given the winner's time. In terms of results, they were ranked in the order they crossed the finish line in. This rule doesn't apply in time trials or stages with summit finish.

Road cycling is an outdoor sport and races cover a very wide area, so things happen that organizers can't foresee.

In 2019 edition of Tour de France, an announcement was made in the middle of the stage, the summit the riders already crossed would count as a finish since the road further on was impassable due to a landslide and hail. It turned out later that this stage decided the winner of the Tour.

During stage five of the Giro 2019, we witnessed an unusual but correct decision from the race commissaíres talking to some (among others to my guy in the pink jersey) riders right from the car; it was decided later to neutralize the stage for the GC nine kilometers before the finish.

It was raining from the start, and there were a few dozen centimeters of water on the road at times. The final part of the stage comprised of a few nine-kilometer laps, each crossing the finish line. Even though everyone had to ride the same number of laps, the GC timer stopped the penultimate time they rode across the finish line. The last lap was exclusively for the sprinters who were in it for the stage win. It was safer for everyone this way. And no fun for anyone.

IF THE PELOTON BREAKS IN HALF DUE TO A RAILROAD CROSSING GATE BEING LOWERED, THE GROUP THAT MANAGED TO AVOID WAITING FOR A TRAIN TO DRIVE BY HAS TO SLOW DOWN OR EVEN STOP SO THE RIDERS WHO GOT STUCK BEHIND THE GATE CAN CATCH UP. THE RACE RETURNS TO THE SITUATION FROM BEFORE THE TRAIN'S ARRIVAL. FOR INSTANCE, THE COMMISSAIRES STOP THE BREAK WHILE THE BUNCH IS WAITING BEHIND THE CROSSING GATE.

There's also something called the UCI extreme weather protocol; it was introduced only in 2016, but it's not quite applicable, as it's not clear who decides about implementing it and when. It states that a stage may be canceled or adjusted. I'm sure you all remember the infamous scene of Chris Froome running without his bicycle on Mont Ventoux. It was so windy on the top they had to lower the finish for about six kilometers. A stage of the Paris-Nice race was once canceled due to snowfall, and one in Dubai due to a sand storm. The rule should be applied sometimes, but it's not because riders and teams oppose; they don't want to miss a chance at a good result if they're well prepared. But the health and safety of riders and spectators are always most important.

Primož rode in Switzerland once:

> ❝ *In one stage of the Tour de Romandie, it was snowing from start to finish. April in the Swiss mountains isn't really toasty. It's dangerous because your fingers freeze and you can't brake. I was spilling hot tea from the team car over my hands in the last part so I could finish the stage. I saw some guys pee on their hands. Well, I wasn't that cold.* ❞

Weather is one of the most influential factors in cycling. Anything can happen to riders on the road anyway, and then there is the weather sometimes deciding a race as well. Especially in the Giro with high mountains and an early slot in the racing calendar, stages were canceled in the past or sometimes they rode through a narrow plowed corridor on snow covered road or during a heavy snowfall. The Tour and the Vuelta are better off as they have much better slots in July and August.

STAGE FIFTEEN

SEPTEMBER 8, 2019

TINEO ·······▶ SANTUARIO DEL ACEBO

154 KM, MOUNTAIN

ROGLIČ AND VALVERDE JOINED FORCES AND ESCAPED THE REST OF THE FAVORITES

[…] One of Primož Roglič's main men in Jumbo-Visma, Sepp Kuss, won stage 15 of the Tour of Spain. The Slovenian ace crossed the finish line together with Alejandro Valverde, and they both extended their advantage over other chasers. […]

Roglič kept his advantage (2:25) over Valverde. Pogačar is third now and 3:42 behind. He kept 17 seconds of advantage over Lopez. Quintana, now fifth, is lagging 5:09 behind Roglič. […]

At the beginning of the third climb, Sergio Samitier (Euskadi-Murias) was the first one from the breakaway group of 17 riders to attack. Four kilometers from the summit of the climb to Puerto del Pozo de las Mujeres Muertas, Ben O'Connor (Dimension Data) and Dani Navarro (Katusha) joined him. At that point, they had a good minute of advantage and over four-minute advantage over the peloton with the red jersey and the rest of the favorites. […]

Kuss jumped from the group of chasers, fiercely accelerating and overtaking Samitier with 6.6 kilometers to go. Meanwhile, the chase fell apart, and the 24 year old American ramped up 30 seconds of advantage in the last five kilometers. […] (RTV MMC 2019n)

SLO 1. ROGLIČ, PRIMOŽ (JUMBO-VISMA)   58:10:32

ESP 2. VALVERDE, ALEJANDRO (MOVISTAR)   +2:25

SLO 3. POGAČAR, TADEJ (UAE TEAM EMIRATES)   +3:42

We often see this sight in a breakaway. If escapees want to be successful, they all have to contribute to the work in the front. Sepp got his instruction from the team car: »Sit on and do nothing.« Don't do anything. Why? Because he can always say, he's waiting for his captain. What we witnessed was a risky move, especially because Sepp was to be Primož's last domestique. Luckily Primož didn't need him. They could've told Sepp to wait for his captain. But when it turned out the bunch could not catch up with the breakaway before the climb, he got free rein.

CIDER IN ASTURIAS

Oviedo, September 8, 2019

After all the drama on Los Machucos, the whole Saturday was intended for logistics. My tribe went home, replacing them were Špela and (another) Primož, and the decision was made –mini Primož and I are going all the way to Madrid. We left Oviedo at sundown. Looking for food, we landed in a typical Asturian restaurant with a huge meat grill, where they poured from a bottle held high in the air a drink called sidra, cider in English. In colloquial Slovenian we call it tolkec, but Rogli would say, »tokuc« and let's say I take his naming as valid.

The waiter hoists the bottle high over his head, while he holds the glass in the other hand as low as he can get it, making the distance between the glass and the bottle as long as possible, and then pours the drink quickly. Foam fills the glass up to the rim, and there are only about three fingers of liquid left. It's an art to hit the glass with the jet, so the floor is all sticky, and you have to down the poured drink at once. He stands at your table and points to the glass, so you have to drink. If you can keep up for a while, you wind up drunk as a skunk.

We did laundry at a laundromat like in American movies the next morning and tried to catch the start of the Tineo stage - semi-successfully. Despite rushing like crazy, Špela and I (plus Lev in his blanket) only saw riders slowly grinding a climb in a départ fictif, before disappearing over a turn. Who sticks a climb into départ fictif? Sadists!

We went to Acebo later. I thought it might be one of the decisive climbs in the race. The stage is due to finish at a monastery atop of some kind of a plateau that looks round and soft and kind. Santuario del Acebo. But while trying to conquer the top, confusion ensues. They already rode the climb in this stage, but on another route than they will for the second time. Špela and I keep pushing the stroller uphill at about 110 °F, the heat radiates from the asphalt, and no sign of a race.

No, no. We turn around, another road, same shit. The third road on the same climb, even hotter and steeper, I'll have a heart attack, I swear. Phones don't work. Lev is not in the mood and whimpers as always when his mother's nervous because a mother and a child are practically the same person in the child's first year of life. Hello, how could you forget? Shit, shit, shit, I don't care, la, la, la, I don't care at this moment if I'm one and a half person! I want to see climbing carnage! I am foaming at the mount in my mind with rage while repeating this to myself. I want to see it!!!

Shit. The first helicopter glides into the U-shaped valley in the distance. They're here; it's over. I wave off briskly. We're trying as hard as we can to get a view of the road down the valley, but all we see is a big group of riders that we assume is the peloton, and a colorful line of cars behind them. The helicopter, now joined by another one, floats to the right end of the valley, then turns around, as if we were watching over a huge tennis court beneath us. Phones still don't work and I am pretty sure the race is already being decided down there. But actually, I'm just so confused, and it takes me a while to realize that one helicopter is tracing the breakaway while the other is following the peloton. The only thing we can do is quickly descend back to the valley and try to find a bar with a TV. If I were a hedgehog, now would be the time to curl into a ball and roll into the valley. But I'm not. Instead of rolling down, I carried my sweet little kitten all the way down, so he finally calmed down, but at the same time, we overheated to the boiling point. Yay!

And because I'm not a hedgehog, and luck isn't always a lady, it's siesta time down there. There's a bar on one of the street corners. It feels as if we went right back to 1968, but it has a tiny TV. Everyone is staring at the screen. Hallelujah! They'll serve us a beer, and they say we can watch with them. Ah, here they are, blurry figures representing riders on the TV screen. The breakaway is coming. Where's my egg yolk in red jersey? He's sticking to the rainbow jersey, as he should.

Everything is OK. One stage less to Madrid, I tell myself every day, and I'm deeply relieved after this one. We toast to a successful day and then wander for at least another hour up and down the road, waiting for both Primožes. Špela's one is here. A little upset, I watch how all of 170 or so riders descend in irregular intervals and relaxed conversation. My heart skips a beat every time I see a sunny yellow color, but he's nowhere to be seen.

For those riding by, the day's work is done. When we gasped, walking aimlessly, we noticed from above a parking lot, packed with team busses. After more than an hour of standing on the sidewalk, and the little one almost getting a hernia from screaming, I'm devastated because I don't know what to do, apart from finally accepting the fact he's not coming. To be fair, deep down, I knew that already, but I hoped anyway it would be different today.

It's like when you're in a breakaway, and you know they'll catch you before the finish line, but you push into the wind anyway. You're bound to succeed one day. The closest we are to one another is when we get stuck in the queue of vehicles, letting his bus pull out of the parking lot. But he's probably not even there. The cycling life sucks, let me tell you.

The team hideaway

STAGE SIXTEEN

SEPTEMBER 9, 2019

PRAVIA ·······> ALTO DE LA CUBILLA LENA

144 KM, MOUNTAIN

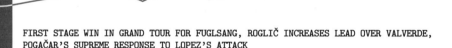

FIRST STAGE WIN IN GRAND TOUR FOR FUGLSANG, ROGLIČ INCREASES LEAD OVER VALVERDE, POGAČAR'S SUPREME RESPONSE TO LOPEZ'S ATTACK

Stage 16 of the Tour of Spain offered a long, teasing foreplay, reaching the climax at the top of the final climb on Cubilla, where Roglič and Pogačar showed their exceptional power once again as the only ones able to follow Lopez's attack.

Jakob Fuglsang was already celebrating his first stage win in Grand Tours when the moment of truth hit the group of favorites. Primož Roglič and Tadej Pogačar managed the situation confidently and responded to the last attack staged by Miguel Lopez, fourth in the GC. […]

Roglič squeezed out the last ounces of strength, even though he could have stayed in Alejandro Valverde's group. But the eagle from Zasavje, constantly surrounded with Jumbo-Visma teammates up to the last few kilometers, didn't let go and was well rewarded for his relentlessness: he extended his lead in the general classification. Valverde finished 23 seconds behind, meaning the world champion is now trailing 2:48 behind Roglič, while Pogačar is third at 3:42 behind. […]

It was one of the few opportunities left to attack, as the remaining Thursday and Saturday stages are the only ones left to offer a possibility of major changes in the general classification. The three-week marathon will end in Madrid on Sunday. (RTV MMC 2019o)

SLO	1. ROGLIČ, PRIMOŽ (JUMBO-VISMA)		62:17:52
ESP	2. VALVERDE, ALEJANDRO (MOVISTAR)		+2:48
SLO	3. POGAČAR, TADEJ (UAE TEAM EMIRATES)		+3:42

The cycling dictionary describes these kinds of guys as all-rounders, an apt description because they are good all-around – everywhere. These are the universal cyclists we'll see fighting for the GC. They are good in the mountains, at time trials, and they don't lose time on the flats. They often find themselves being captains in one-day or in stage races. A rider can win the general classification even without winning a single stage.

We can loosely sort riders into different categories according to the type of terrain where they feel most at home.

We already know where the climbers shine – in the mountains. Or better put, on climbs. But riders are just as different as incline profiles are; some are better on gentle slopes, while others thrive at higher altitudes. And some prefer steeper climbs.

Punchers are riders who are strongest on the short and steep climbs, the kind of climbs we see in spring classics.

Mur de Huy[43] is a good example - only 1.3 km long, with an average grade of 9.3 percent and a maximum grade of 26 percent. The Mur, which means wall, is the traditional finish of La Flèche Wallonne, one of Belgium's most famous classics. Contrary to climbers, punchers are explosive and closer to sprinters than real *grimpeurs*. We find some sprinters among punchers, but not typical ones who can only sprint following a perfect lead-out on flats.

Sprint specialists are the strongest riders in the bunch. They develop huge power in (and for) a very short time, which is the most important thing for nailing a finish with the right timing. Because they're built differently (they have more muscle), their watts-to-kilograms ratio is too low to enjoy climbing.

---

[43] Pronounced Mur de wi.

If we go back to this book's beginning, we probably remember classics are special one-day events, either with short, steep climbs or with many cobbled sections and dirt roads. Or with everything above. In long and challenging races like Paris–Roubaix, with many cobbled sections, we'll most likely find our winner among the *rouleurs*. This is a poetic French name for riders who are very strong on flats and challenging terrains (cobbles, mud, and dirt roads).

The French have their jargon when it comes to cycling, and the whole world takes it from them.

They also have an expression for a rider who is often in a breakaway and, literally translated, it means an adventurer. A *baroudeur* will try in very romantic and dramatic French fashion to go all the way, even though we know that most of the riders in breakaways are aware of the possibility of being unsuccessful when they, full of hope, lunge into an attack. That's why, when they feel the peloton breathing down their neck and

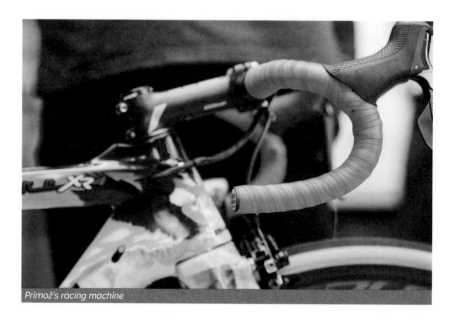

Primož's racing machine

they realize that their time might be up, they'll often shake hands and finish their relatively successful or unsuccessful day with a fist bump.

There are also time trial specialists in the peloton swarm. Time trialists are extremely strong riders, less explosive, but with more stamina than sprinters, so they're also pretty well revered as domestiques.

And as much as riders are different, so are bikes. We've already discussed the time trial bikes and »simple« road bikes. For the latter we could say they are all-rounders, much like riders who can hold their own on every terrain.

Primož also has a bike, specially made for climbing. He says it's lighter and stiffer (those who ride will know what that means), and less aerodynamic. The frame is not varnished, which means lower weight, but also a slower bike. The handlebars and the saddle are different, too. Everything is designed for the bike to be lighter.

Then there are bikes with features to soften the ride on cobbles and dirt roads. They are heavier, and you can fit wider tires on their rims, so they perform better on off-road terrain.

The bike's characteristics depend mostly on its gear. I'm talking about handlebars, crank size, and wheels. The gears are important, too – the better part of the peloton uses an electronic shifting

THE BIKE WEIGHT HAS A LOWER LIMIT. WITH ALL THE EQUIPMENT, IT MUST NOT BE LIGHTER THAN 6.8 KG. IN THE EARLY DAYS OF THE TOUR DE FRANCE, BIKES WERE A LOT HEAVIER.

system. Brakes have changed considerably in the last years. Since 2017, disc brakes are allowed in WT races, making bikes heavier, but braking is more responsive, especially in bad weather, faster and more effective. The pro peloton was reluctant to use disc brakes for a long time due to the danger of cuts and burns in massive crashes.

Bikes are fitted with special devices that allow us to know what's happening during races. And not only in races. They are extremely useful in the training process, where experts and coaches consider carefully every miniscule statistic available thanks of those tiny devices.

So it's not just about stubborn pedal pushing? Amateur riders will probably never ask that question. Never ever. The basic device they have on their handlebars is a cycle computer; let's call it that even though it has a bunch of names. It tracks your course, speed, heart rate, air temperature, elevation, cadence[44], and a whole lot of other stuff, depending on how powerful it is. Professional riders see on their screen at least one other variable – power. A power meter is often fitted to the crank.

If you've ever ridden a sportive, you know you need a special chip to measure time. The same goes for elite road races where the chip is fitted to the front forks.

When a number of riders cross the finish line tightly packed together, which happens mostly in sprints, a photo finish decides the winner. The first one to touch the finish line with the front wheel wins.

A newer device for tracking data that came about mostly for spectators is a sort of a beacon some riders[45] have fitted under their saddles. It sends live data to available media, and fans can track speed, power, cadence, heart rate, position in the race, and a few other stats in real-time. Glitches in this thingamajig cause much stress and uncertainty to emotionally involved subjects, such as myself. A speed of zero on Primož's transmitter when he should be riding at 45 km/h within the group? If I don't immediately have a stroke, I'm already calling the sports director in the team vehicle.

---

[44] Cadence is the number of the crank revolutions per minute.
[45] Only riders in teams that have contracts with the manufacturer of such device.

Little screens are a bond between a bike in a rider

Cameras, occasionally fitted under saddles or on handlebars of some riders, also provide interesting inside information. They allow us to see the dynamic events during the race. We see how dramatic riding in the peloton is, and we hear many things we wouldn't otherwise.

ALTO DE LA CUBILLA

Just this one and two more, and then we're done. From now on, I'm only counting mountain stages. But I know just enough about cycling now it should be obvious to me that I shouldn't do that. This hill looks more or less French on the map, so I hope the road is a bit better and there's more space on the top. But the climb is very long. The camper drives about as fast as the riders will. Driving up, we pick up two Slovenians that are walking towards the top. We are surrounded by green, vast, open space, but the

road inspires less and less confidence as we keep edging to its end. Luckily, we only get stuck between fences in the finish area. They can pull us from here, I think.

A gentle descent behind the finish extends into a soft green plateau. There are wooden fences everywhere, and a stone house that looks like a mountain lodge. There are horses out and the weather is weird. The wind pushes a thick mist of clouds among the peaks every now and then, and at last, it just stays there. It's very peaceful.

For the first time, I see an Anatolian Shepherd Dog anywhere else than in our home garden.

Our dog Hač is just like this devil. Let me rephrase this: he's not a dog because he's really a horse. Or at least of a similar size. His magnificent hairy figure would make someone who didn't know better think that it's a runaway polar bear. Otherwise, Hač is the only Turk in my hometown of Hoče that I know of.

Hač's older relatives on Cubilla are more unkempt and with the famous claw, maybe a little bit smaller than him, and there's a mule with a wooden saddle tied to a dwarf pine. I kid you not.

Hačes are watching over horses. The closer riders are to the top, the thicker the fog gets. It's so thick by the end that I see nothing. I can barely see the screen. He doesn't have the legs for it, I can see that. I just hope it's not too bad. The fog is wet, and it sticks to my face. And the wind blows like hell. Lev's asleep in his stroller. I gently stroke his little head every now and then just to remind myself that nothing else matters.

The clouds are like cotton that the wind rolls around the ground. Primož catches up to those in front before the finish. It ends, and tomorrow is a rest day. We wait for him next to his team van while the crowd spills in all directions – some going up, some descending back down. I'm standing by bike 131 when he drags himself towards me with a bunch of people waving their phones behind him.

❝ Jesus, there were hard climbs before this one. There was a huge breakaway, and we controlled it, but we were riding too hard. Five hundred watts at 20 kilometers to the finish line. Our guys went berserk. I tried to tell them to pull with some sense because they'll be attacking at the end. I had to ride tempo at the end to salvage it. ❞ *He could easily*

leave out those numbers as far as I'm concerned. But he's relieved, and tomorrow they won't have to think too much. You and your tempo, I think to myself. Whatever.

A helicopter tries to land in the fog, but it knocks over the tent where the riders give statements after the stage. It takes an eternity to get to the road. Somewhere in Spain's nameless mountains that remind me of France, another day went by beside Hačes wrapped in clouds. The next stop, Burgos. A rest day.

REST DAY

SEPTEMBER 10, 2019

Burgos, September 10, 2019

When we drove into the parking lot yesterday, only a few lights were on in the hotel. Which room is he in? Busses are standing motionless in front of the entrance, surrounded by team vehicles, shining in the luminescence of tall street lights, even though they will be washed again before they move on. We'll sleep in the parking lot in front of their hotel.

It's the second rest day in the Tour of Spain. And the last one. That means we're close. The wind was blowing hard the whole night through, shaking stuff from the tree we parked under on the roof of our mobile home.

We woke up to an unexpectedly cold summer morning. Mister Polska, the team's swanny, left some fresh bread and prosciutto for us in the camper's trunk. Mister Maillot Rojo also dropped by, dressed for training, to spend a few moments with his descendant. We were killing time in the hotel lobby and the bar. It was not pleasant outside. I spent my day swapping coffee for mineral water and that for orange juice.

Then I washed my hair in the hotel room while my guys were rolling around the bed. A moment of family bliss in the vortex of a hectic three-week race. We had 30 minutes left, but it was so cold that I dressed my little one and myself with everything we had, and it still wasn't enough. We sat in the camper wrapped in blankets and with coffee in our hands, eyes glued to the little TV screen, replaying the stage from the day before until the time came for him to take care of other duties. It's impossible to step out of the loop, even if for just a moment. The day is suddenly over.

I watch washed and shiny busses drive off the parking lot the next day, and I wave goodbye. Then, we stuff ourselves into the camper, and just as we want to leave the parking lot, the police stop us. Špela hasn't put her safety belt on yet. That warrants a traffic ticket, says the policeman, while I'm lying on the bed under the window in the back of the camper, trying not to let on that I'm there, hoping Lev doesn't make a sound.

STAGE SEVENTEEN

SEPTEMBER 11, 2019

ARANDA DE DUERO ·······► GUADALAJARA

220 KM, HILLY

ROGLIČ SURVIVES QUINTANA'S ATTACK, POGAČAR LOSES ONE PLACE

Stage win for Philippe Gilbert of Belgium. […] The undulating, 219-kilometer long course between Aranda de Duero and Guadalajara in central Spain was marked with an early breakaway of about 30 riders, including Quintana, sitting in sixth before stage 17, and almost eight minutes behind the race leader. The escape with the Movistar riders at the helm dictated a punishing tempo benefiting from some help from the wind, making it impossible for the peloton, Roglič and Pogačar included, to bring them back.

The breakaway's advantage was rising quickly. The Slovenians, who were left without their teammates, suffered and reached the finish as 30th and 31st, more than five minutes behind the Belgian stage winner Philippe Gilbert. Roglič successfully defended the red jersey, while Quintana drew nearer and is now placed second, two minutes and 24 seconds behind. Alejandro Valverde of Spain is third (+2:48), Pogačar is fourth (+3:42).

The stage was the fastest in this race history, with an average speed of 50.6 km/h.

SLO 1. ROGLIČ, PRIMOŽ (JUMBO-VISMA)	66:43:36
COL 2. QUINTANA, NAIRO (MOVISTAR)	+2:24
ESP 3. VALVERDE, ALEJANDRO (MOVISTAR)	+2:48

That was intense! 50.6 km/h is like riding a vespa! A very long stage and the suffer-fest began practically at kilometer zero. Zero is a relative concept in cycling. How is this possible, you ask?

Before riders hop on their carbon horses, they go to the sign-in. There's a board, often made of glass, stating starting numbers of all the riders on a large stage, usually in the town center. Every rider must sign their name next to their number. If they don't, they're subject to penalty. Lately, the commissars even dish out penalties for being late to signing. But there is no sign-in before a time trial.

When they're done, they hop on their bikes under the stage and ride under an inflatable arc where the race director's vehicle and motorbikes are waiting. The first row is designated to jersey holders, and stars organizers want to show off, mostly the world champion and winners of big races. In Italy and France, they'll push forward one of their own, which is appropriate, of course.

And here comes the trick. The gun goes off, and riders start spinning the pedals, still having a laugh at the peloton's rear end, and greeting the spectators. What's the catch? Why are they dragging themselves so slowly? Why don't they lunge like hungry pigs into pumpkins?

The starting gunshot doesn't mean the real start. Road races have a so-called flying start. They start in a town center because of spectators, but roads there are too dangerous for a real fight, so the road they cover from *départ fictif* to the kilometer zero is a so-called neutral zone. The leisurely ridden kilometers are not calculated into the stage length. So those poor souls rode 219 kilometers plus a few more in the neutral zone in stage seventeen! The length of the neutral ride is written in the roadbook.

When they reach kilometer zero, the race director waves a start flag from his car, and then comes the *départ réel* – the actual start. At that moment, the race begins and first attacks with it. We already know that it takes some time for the breakaway to form. But, as we'll see now, it's not always like that.

At the very beginning of stage seventeen, a big group of about 30 excellent riders attacked, and so instead of an escape, we had two pelotons on the road.

Where was the yellow team? Even though everyone knew that some teams would launch multiple attacks trying to break up the bunch with the help of crosswinds - especially riders from Benelux have that in their blood - no one expected it to happen immediately at the white flag's flutter. Our canaries were asleep at the rear of the peloton. They didn't have anyone in the front group. And that's where the problem occurs. The

Riders in the neutral zone and the race director's car

Jumbo-Visma riders were faced with a very difficult job. The team with the red jersey holder has the most to lose, possibly even the lead, so it's expected to bear the biggest responsibility for controlling the race.

TV broadcasts are very deceptive in such cases. Viewers will often see the last part of the stage, but they won't have any idea about what went down earlier. That's why we have to always bear in mind what could've occurred in four hours that had already passed before they came to the part we see on TV.

So on that day, with a lot of action from the very beginning, no one had seen Jumbo working at the front of the bunch for the first 120 kilometers. The majority of viewers saw the red jersey alone in the last two hours of the broadcast, thinking another team was saving it. Which is not true – everyone is trying to save themselves.

A breakaway with quite a few excellent riders is hard to control, let alone to catch. They also had the wind on their side, blowing into their backs and helping them ride faster. If it blows from the opposite direction, it builds a wall.

In the wind that blows from behind, the breakaway rider can ride faster while using up less energy, and they can go as fast as 60 km/h. The peloton, in the meanwhile, can't ride 75 or 80 km/h to reduce the gap in the usual pattern of gaining one minute in every ten kilometers.

The wind is a funny thing. It can be the rider's most bitter enemy when it blows from the front, but it can be his greatest ally when they share the same direction.

BY THE WAY, AT 2642 METERS ASL, COL DU GALIBIER WAS THE HIGHEST POINT OF THE 2018 TDF – THE HIGHEST POINT IN THE TOUR IS ALWAYS NAMED SOUVENIR HENRI DESGRANGE, AND THE FIRST RIDER TO CROSS IT WINS A SPECIAL AWARD. IN THE GIRO, THE TOP OF THE RACE IS CALLED CIMA COPPI.

Do you remember the historic first win for Slovenia in the Tour de France when Roglič shot over the monstrous Galibier pass with 30 kilometers to go, mostly downhill? The descent was not a very fast or steep one, so riding down required a lot of work. Two TV commentators were absolutely sure he wouldn't make it, especially because there was a group of very skilled descenders working well together behind him. If the cyclists work together, they can gain a lot by drafting.

Only a few of you, those who have a photographic memory, will remember that Primož crashed in that stage when the road was already climbing slightly, thanks to his silly mistake. The only consequences were a momentary loss of contact with the group and the chain slipping off the gearwheel.

Even fewer will remember he mended the chain by himself despite his team car being there - the breakaway he was a part of had a few minutes on the peloton, hence he had the team car practically behind his back.

Truth be told, the guy is a little bit odd. But to the extent of not wanting another bike? Here comes the catch. His backup bike had a smaller chainring with a smaller number of teeth (beats me how you count those things), and he wanted to ride the bike with a bigger one in case

> ❝ *I go for a solo descent from Lautaret and there's headwind, then I won't have to grind that much.* ❞

Namely, the bigger the chainring in the front, the faster you go with less effort. Primož had 54 teeth on that particular bike.

Hm. The boy was thinking. And as it happens, there was in fact a headwind and he did indeed go for a solo descent.

On top of that, he knew the road well – we had vacationed for 14 days in a town in a valley close by about a month before the race. He rode that descent almost every day, familiarized himself with the weather patterns, and used that knowledge in the race. Every afternoon the wind that ski jumpers would call an updraft was blowing towards the huge snow-covered peaks.

When he called me that morning before the stage, I was just getting on my bike in Serre Chevalier. He asked me where exactly the finish line was and added that he'd be coming alone – I was in tears immediately. He said to wait for him at the finish because he'd win. I didn't even dare to think something like that would happen to us and that we would share that moment with countless fans who slept in drenched tents by the road just to see their heroes for a few seconds. It was too much for me. My euphoria spilled over the edge of my eyes. I was about a kilometer from the finish line a few hours later, hesitating. He was in the breakaway, but so were a lot of other big names.

When the decisive attack came, I said to myself only a complete idiot would do something like that. Attacking solo more than 30 kilometers from the finish line warrants that kind of verdict. But he refuted all predictions and theories, of course, and I was more and more drawn towards the finish line. Getting there on that day was something like trying to get into the Pentagon because his *monsieur* the French president was in attendance as well. The guy who was having a beer at the table next to ours at the bar the evening before had needed to remove the cattle from his field to let the presidential helicopter land there. The Savoy Alps are a lucky place for us. Later that day, when he had already written history, the past, and the future, I didn't cry. Did I even dare to imagine he had put me at the finish of the queen stage of Tour de France because he simply said he'd win?

Anyway, back to technical stuff. Considering his win, we can conclude that repairing chain by himself was a good decision.

There's another type of wind that makes some riders shudder in fear – wind from the side. In cycling lingo that's a crosswind. When forecasted, everyone knows it will be a rough ride sooner or later. Classics riders will try to split the peloton.

But with the crosswind, splitting the peloton into smaller groups is something of an art form. For the system to break down, you need the help of a cross tailwind to reach high speed. And then comes the big moment – one or more echelons, diagonal formations, appear.

Even riders themselves have a hard time understanding how they come about sometimes.

For the GC riders who are in it for a good result in the general classification, riding in echelons is much more challenging than climbs. Climbs are always in the same place, and riders can prepare for them. On the other hand, riding in the crosswind is a lovely bundle of surprises. Everyone knows something will happen, but no one knows when; they have to be alert every second, so they don't miss the decisive move. It usually comes where the road is flat and open, with nothing providing any cover to the riders.

Riders position themselves over the road in a diagonal line. Then they rotate into the wind. When an echelon is formed, you're better off cooperating and doing your part at the front, or you might find yourself thrown out at the back; because the formation is positioned diagonally to the road edges, there's not enough room for everybody. When a team decides to make a selection using the wind, it rides in front and starts riding hard. It rides at the edge of the road, thus taking up space from riders who'd want to draft. This kind of riding is a specialty of teams coming from countries with a lot of open terrain where riders are used to crosswinds.

It's a complicated thing, and no rider wants to stay behind in these kinds of situations, least of all alone. If they do fall off in the crosswind, they'll have to endure quite a bit of torture and probably won't catch up with the group.

Echelons are especially interesting for viewers, and not really popular with the riders. Trying to keep up in a crosswind on open flats is particularly challenging for lightweight[46], thin riders, and many times it can be even harder than climbing.

---

[46] This is not always the case, and sometimes they manage to sneak through somehow. We saw some excellent climbers in the front group in stage 17 of the Vuelta.

THE WINDY ROCK 'N' ROLL

Guadalajara, September 11, 2019

It finally dawns on me what it reminds me of. Our evenings were different on the Croatian island of Pag in our holiday cabin until we finally got electricity a few years ago. We always sat on the front patio with a sea view in the pitch dark and gazed at the stars. There's not another house in view, so we saw millions of them. It was almost like looking at scattered glittering grains, spreading into eternity. Then we would look at moving dots in the sky and make bets about where they were flying.

»This one is flying to Moscow. Oh, Greece, for sure. Maybe Malta?« But the most special were evenings with my neighbor and her guitar. It's a memory I can hear in my head. My grandma always wanted her to play Negrete's Jalisco, but the rendition by Serbian singer Predrag Gojković. I was sure Jalisco was a horse, a shiny black stallion. But Jalisco is a state in Mexico.

Predrag Gojković sings about it:

> *Ay, Jalisco, Jalisco, Jalisco,*
> *The whole world knows you and Guadalajara,*
> *Your beauty, and the fire in your heart,*
> *And the glow within the song is with you.*
> *Ay, Jalisco, the land of dreams,*
> *There's hope within you, there's magic within you,*
> *And the fire of life, and joy, and happiness*
> *For you when asked to, one can even give his life.*

And there it was, Guadalajara. Not the one from that song, and there was no old generator rumbling under the terrace, and there were no stars to be seen. The wind was blowing in weird gusts, swirling sand in the air, spraying a thin layer of it over the camper's windows. We were close to our destination. The longest stage of this year's Vuelta. Guadalajara in the autonomous community of Castilla–La Mancha near Madrid.

Dry plateaus without any considerable greenery by the highway can only mean one thing – the wind. You asked for it, so here it is: crosstail wind, ideal conditions for echelons.

But that all the hell would break loose so soon? I would never have guessed. We stare at the TV, completely clenched. I have the feeling I'm hearing droplets of time falling into an abyss, echoing their plop, plop, plop.

He could lose the jersey. He could lose the Vuelta. He's alone. Everyone who fucked up is trying to save their seconds. They're taking turns. It doesn't look good.

I exchange couple of texts with Vinko while the wind wants to shatter our dreams: »The ingenious gentleman, Don Quixote of La Mancha.«

»What?« I'm not in the mood for these jokes. And he knows talking to me during the race is like trying to teach a horse how to speak French, so kindly go to hell.

»Well, he fought windmills. The whole peloton should read that book. Well, at least the ones stuck behind.«

The provoker of all of my emotional states. My brain is in a cortisol marinade at the moment, don't horse around.

»I don't understand. And I really don't feel like it now.«

»He was from La Mancha! The wind has been blowing here for the last 600 years, duh!«

Finally, it ends. The bunch, if you can call it that because the red jersey is in it, finished with a considerable time gap. While we were all thinking about mountains, we were almost blown off the flats. We meet at the fence after everything is already cleared and he's leaving. The wind is trying to yank the flag from my hands. He's shaking his head, coughing, and his face is almost as red as the jersey he's wearing. He's covered in dust, and his eyes are bloodshot.

I whistle Jalisco to myself on our way back to the camper. Ay, Jalisco, Jalisco, there's hope within you, there's magic within you … Blah, blah, blah, crowned with glory, fiery Jalisco.

Will my knight be crowned with glory? If I ever have a black horse, I'll name it Jalisco. That's the resolution I make there, in the windy Guadalajara.

STAGE EIGHTEEN

SEPTEMBER 12, 2019

COLMENAR VIEJO ·······▶ BECERRIL DE LA SIERRA

178 KM, MOUNTAIN

ONLY HIGUITA IN FRONT OF ROGLIČ IN STAGE 18, POGAČAR SURRENDERS THE WHITE JERSEY
TO LOPEZ […]

Primož Roglič is much closer to the overall win in the Tour of Spain. He came in
second in stage 18 and was faster in the finish sprint than his biggest rival,
Alejandro Valverde. […]

Riders had to deal with four climbs of Category 1 in the 177.5-kilometer stage
18 from Colmenar Viejo to Becerril de la Sierra. Sergio Higuita was riding in
the breakaway of the day and celebrated the biggest success of his career. It
was the first win in the professional peloton for the 22-year-old Colombian. […]

Lopez attacked on the climb, hunting the podium and the white jersey. The first
few attacks didn't amount to success, but he finally made it 30 kilometers before
the finish. Roglič and Valverde managed to follow, while Nairo Quintana and
Pogačar didn't. […]

Roglič grappled with Valverde in the sprint for second place in the stage and
bonus seconds and succeeded. He increased his advantage for two more seconds
and has two minutes and 50 seconds lead over the Spaniard. […] (RTV MMC 2019r)

SLO 1. ROGLIČ, PRIMOŽ (JUMBO-VISMA)   71:16:54
ESP 2. VALVERDE, ALEJANDRO (MOVISTAR)   +2:50
COL 3. QUINTANA, NAIRO (MOVISTAR)   +3:31

keep mentioning time differences in the general classification. But can a rider with no ambition in mountain stages or the general classification ride his own tempo to the finish like walking in the park?

Forget it! A race is a race, and it's a race for everyone.

All riders must finish within a designated time limit, calculated based on the winner's time, or they're disqualified.

When someone finishes outside of the time limit and is disqualified, the French add HD to his name. And no, it's not a fancy HD TV. It means *hors délai*, outside the time limit – out of time. They just love to use the word *hors*, don't they?

I heard once there's a sprinter on the bus. »Did he crash?« I asked because I thought they were talking about a team bus. No. The bus is also a term for a group of riders in a stage ride, mostly domestiques who have already done their part and sprinters or climbing non-specialists, working together in a group with only one goal in mind – to finish within the time limit. They are usually far behind the peloton. The Italian word for this little bunch of merry riders, also widely used all over the world, is *gruppetto*. We might also call it a disco group.

And how do the organizers calculate who stays in the race? Do they say, if the stage begins at noon, we'll wait until seven in the evening and then just pack up and leave?

The French are much too fastidious for something like that. There is a formula for calculating who stays and who goes, but, on the other hand, this is one of those things in the TDF that are kind of approximate. The rules state the time limit depends on the stage speed and difficulty.

On a flat and slow (as if...) stage with an average speed lower than 36 km/h, the maximum lag may not exceed 3% of the winner's time. The permitted percentage goes up to 22 in the event of a very fast or a mountain stage. In time trials, we get even to a quarter; riders need to finish within winner's time plus 25%. So they have a whole time trial to calculate how far behind they're allowed to be.

On average, lags of about 15% are allowed for hilly stages with an undulating profile. A time limit is calculated separately for every stage.

But the French wouldn't be the French if they didn't do everything the French way. Sometimes riders who are important for the race's image find themselves in a gruppetto, and the commissaires want them to stay in the race for publicity. A gruppetto is lucky on days like that. Except when it's not.

At the tail of the caravan, behind everyone else, we find the broom wagon. A van sweeping the road (many times with an actual broom stuck behind one of the side mirrors, so everyone knows its role), but metaphorically. This vehicle has some work, mostly in amateur and lower-ranked races. I heard it sometimes picks up riders that can't continue the race.

> ❝ *I have no idea what the broom does. I'm sure it never picked me up. They probably have some panels in there, some equipment. It's not really important in the big races. But it's always there, yes, the last in the convoy.* ❞

BULLFIGHTERS

Colmenar Viejo, September 12, 2019

We're very close to Madrid, and I'm losing more and more sleep. Our logistics is now at a high level and we're a well-oiled machine. Every evening we position ourselves at the start of the next day's stage, get into a heated discussion with at least three police officers on average, knock over a few fences, etc. We always make it. Here, we got stuck only at the start. I jumped out barefooted with a shirt over my backside, moved the fence quickly, and closed the road again before the policeman managed to turn around and join the ranks of those who had the luck to get into a fight with me. He was lucky.

Our camper draws a lot of attention, and many look through the window to see if el lider *is in it.*

No, he's not. There's a cranky brat who doesn't want to sleep along with a couple of normal people and a female nervous wreck with a crick in the neck, back, and shoulders and who's terrified of the next three days. While the kid can be like an angel, well occasionally, I'm constantly snappy.

The next day is hot and dry. The town is meh, so we're very happy when we see some busses reeling in, cramming around the corners like ginormous creatures. The Colombians run after them even before they stop. They live for cycling.

I drank too many coffees, and I have a thin layer of dust on my glasses, again. Is this Madrid in the desert? I'm sending messages like crazy; do you see us, do you? It's not difficult to spot us; I know it's not, but he's disconnected, Rogli out.

We wait in front of the bus for some time, blending in with other cycling fans. When he steps out, people go crazy like he's a god. He walks up to us, but we don't speak much. Everyone is staring at us like we're a rare species in a terrarium, like a yellow Burmese python, or a 15-kilo mortadella at the village grocery store, a wonder that everyone has to see, a reality show. There are a gazillion phones over just as many heads.

I don't even know what to say. How's it goin'? I know he's half dead. The weather's good, right? So, what you're having for lunch today? Coke, two energy gels, and a sandwich with some caffeine? So I rather say nothing.

He leaves quickly because everyone on the inside of the circle is uncomfortable, and no one is thinking about how fragile the three-month-old tucked between us is. I'm sick and tired of having to share him with the world.

Someone from the team brings me coffee. The red jersey is distant, but then, for me he is always red, red as the color of love. He's warming up on bike rollers, which means there will be no joking around – full gas from the start. Two policemen wait for him stalwartly. They blow their whistles relentlessly and push their way through the crowd while accompanying him to the signing stage.

This is it. Another battle we have to survive. Hold on, I say with my eyes, bring it home. He understands.

The places I pushed the stroller to over the past two days were stunning. The hills and dales it overcame with a bit of forcing were made for wilderness survival show.

Towards the end of the stage black and yellow team aggressively covers every single attack that could pose an obstacle. Yesterday's lesson was an effective one. At the finish, we're close to a steely bullfight arena where matadors fought dramatically a long time ago. Dressed in red? If not, at least with a red scarf. Passion, romance, eternal love, a myth.

I'm sure someone had been yelling from the stands of the dusty past like we did that day from the other side of the fence. But in the arenas it was always about survival, and maybe we see riders as matadors. Some are red, and others have horns. They all fight. Proudly. Time is their bull.

When I see him defeat the world champion with an unflinching sprint for second place, I know we'll get to Madrid. I desperately need castanets and a red dress.

STAGE NINETEEN

SEPTEMBER 13, 2019

ÁVILA ·······▶ TOLEDO

165 KM, HILLY

ROGLIČ CRASHES AND STRUGGLES, BUT ULTIMATELY EVERYTHING IS UNDER CONTROL [...]

It was another tough day in the Vuelta for Primož Roglič, as he found himself crashing 65 kilometers before the finish. Still, finishing 10th, he retained an almost three-minute advantage over Spaniard Alejandro Valverde, who came in 5th. [...]

The crash was followed by an unsportsmanlike move from the Movistar team led by the GC contender Valverde. They gained a one-minute advantage instead of waiting for the red jersey to get back on his bike and join the peloton as cycling etiquette would have it.

Later, Movistar recognized their mistake and waited for the 29-year rider from Kisovec and others, so all the favorites rode the last 50 kilometers to the finish together. Roglič crossed the finish line in Toledo 10th, Tadej Pogačar took 8th place, and Valverde came in 5th. [...] Roglič kept two minutes and 50 seconds of his advantage over Valverde, with Saturday's decisive stage still to come. [...] (RTV MMC 2019s)

SLO 1. ROGLIČ, PRIMOŽ (JUMBO-VISMA)	75:00:36	
ESP 2. VALVERDE, ALEJANDRO (MOVISTAR)	+2:50	
COL 3. QUINTANA, NAIRO (MOVISTAR)	+3:31	

The common thread in cycling is pain – and that's the truth. Be it the pain that cyclists consciously take on or some other pain, caused for instance by unwanted crashes. For those who remain in our memory for the sacrifices they made to be crowned with a win, wading through oceans of pain is at least rewarded handsomely.

But someone who's not a professional rider can't possibly understand how resilient they are. Tyler Hamilton crashed in stage four of the Giro in 2002 and broke his collar bone; it's one of the most common injuries in cycling. He continued to ride. Not only that – after three weeks of racing, he finished second in the general classification. And that's not the end of the story either. He rode in such pain that he was constantly grinding his teeth, ending up with eleven teeth in such state he had to get porcelain implants.

The American is not the only such case, not even by far. Many of you might remember the Tour de France of 2011. It was a hot day on a very open terrain in the stage to Saint-Flour and five riders were in a breakaway. A TV vehicle trying to avoid a tree veered suddenly and knocked over one of the breakaway riders, who subsequently knocked over another rider, who flew off the road and ended up in a barbed-wire fence. The unfortunate guy who sustained deep cuts, plus 33 stitches after the stage, was Dutch Johnny Hoogerland. Despite being in one of the Tour's most horrific accidents, he finished the stage and later completed the race.

And in this very stage of the Vuelta, where our hopes were almost dashed when the red jersey flew over a wall, our Tony Martin got beaten up the most. The German had to abandon, but I heard that he joked that very evening, with something like 27 stitches on his face, how sorry he was having to leave them.

There is much evidence of riders' resilience. Even first-hand evidence. Years ago, Primož sent me a message from a race on the Croatian

coast, saying he crashed and scratched his face a bit. The next day, he underwent a maxillofacial procedure and had a titanium plate put in under his eye.

When he crashed into a pile of stones while descending in the Sierra Nevada before the Tour de France, he adamantly maintained,

❝ it's nothing, ❞

after slicing off some hip tissue that was dangling through a hole in his shorts. Only later, after the Tour, I accidentally touched his elbow and he howled like a cat with a broken foot being stomped on.

Only after the Tour and four weeks of racing, including the Tour of Slovenia, which he won, they managed to pull a pebble out of an infected wound full of puss on his elbow. A pebble!

❝ Yeah, but it's nothing! ❞

The last person I'll mention here is (how fitting) Lawson Craddock. If you remember my story about the number 13 at the beginning, the symbolic meaning is doubled here. The poor guy turned his number 13 upside down during the Tour of 2018, but that didn't save him from some truly immense bad luck. He was involved in a terrible crash in the first stage and sustained a broken shoulder bone and laceration above his left eye. But that didn't stop him. Three weeks later, he rode to Champs-Élysées in Paris as last in the general classification[47]. Even standing at the start of the Tour is a huge achievement, but finishing the race is even bigger. It doesn't matter if you finish last. The *lanterne rouge* or red lantern is the nickname for the last rider in the Tour de France general classification. The name originates from times when red lanterns marked the rear carriage of a train.

Cycling loves tragic heroes who don't give up. A dignified defeat might not really be a defeat. A special jersey was awarded to the last rider in the Giro general classification for a while – a black one. The last *maglia nera* was awarded in 1951, and the last to get it was Giovanni Pinarello. Sounds familiar? In 1952 he opened a company and started to make bikes. They're still considered to be some of the best.

---

[47] His suffering had a charitable aspect to it. He was trying to raise money to renovate the ruined velodrome in his home town.

EAGLES AND FLYING JERSEYS

Toledo, September 13, 2019

The view of the city sends me back to the Middle Ages. I feel as if we're traveling all the time, and we get there after dark. There's a castle with four turrets on the top of the hill where the city is, much like a castle from a Disney movie. Layers of switchback-like ramparts are baring themselves in the light coming from pavement lights, and to the left there's a stone arch bridge with two guardhouses crossing the river.

I have no idea where we are anymore because we're jumping from one province to another, and everything is close to Madrid. We check every parking app there is, but all the parking lots are full. We're a bit late to the party.

We join the convoy of race vehicles incognito and rush up a narrow climb, already fenced off for tomorrow's stage. The climb is too short and too easy for Primož, I think to myself when we reach the top. Paved with fine cobbles. They say there's no parking here. Of course, they don't know where to put us. We lower the side window, and some jefe really struggles to come up with a solution about what to do with us. The sticker is the right one, yes, »pero grande, no.« He is flapping his arms, pointing at the magnitude of our vehicle.

When another nice policeman calls about half of the police station over a walkietalkie, he decides he doesn't know what to do, either. We're helpless. We start descending from the hill at a snail's pace, and suddenly a police vehicle with flashing lights overtakes us. We wonder for a while if we should follow it. In the end, there's nothing else the police can do but open a secure parking lot. The team busses will be here tomorrow; I get that. And us, obviously. Considering our size, we fit the bill.

The next day, after a sunny morning, the rain came in. It was coming and going whimsically, but the castle had a foggy cap the whole time, threatening to bring some more rain. Narrow streets have some stores where we kill some time, and there's a bronze statue of Federico Bahamontes on a bike at one of the scenic overlooks. He's standing on his pedals. I know he is one

of the greatest climbers of all time, and he was called El Águila de Toledo
– the Eagle of Toledo. Judging by the year of his birth, he's no longer alive.

*The city is like an open air museum. I swear I could hear the stomping of
horses carrying knights in their saddles. But instead on that of the knights,
I was waiting the whole day on the sound of the helicopter's roar. And boy
did I hear it. I shuddered at the same time – there were raindrops on the
camera's lens in the air.*

*There were remnants of something living shaped like bushes, streamed in
lines on yellow scorched earth, and on top of them rain. Not much greenery
– it only appears higher up. A recipe for disaster, dry, dusty roads, sprinkled
with water from above; it's going to be as slippery as an ice rink.*

*I forget about that after a while. It's a beautiful day where we're at; we're
having fun, everything's cool. I'm having* café con leche *and* zumo de
naranja. *The rain stops and then starts to fall again, but it's not bothersome.*

*Then, something happens. I fervently wish with all my heart that he's not
there, but at the same time, I'm sure he is. They crashed all over the road.
It's very serious. The only thing I'm capable of is clenching my jaw to the
point of pain under my ear. A deafening clatter. Anxious pain spreads from
the nape of my neck to my pelvis.*

*Five Jumbo-Visma riders crashed; one of them flew into a somersault, and
the other four are jumbled in some kind of a cluster atop one another. The
red jersey flew over a wall. I see him stumbling about among those still on
the ground. The sound that emerges when carbon collides with bodies and
concrete is … There's no word for it; it's indescribable and horrifying. Always.*

*There's a lost shoe that flew off someone's foot lying in the middle of the
road. The TV is showing bare bloody butts and backs. Some manage to
avoid the pileup, others build their own pyre of catastrophe by the low wall
on the other side. Jumbo don't have five spare bikes on their first team car.
I see Primož's red handlebars under a pile of wheels. In pure panic, pushing
the button on the radio, screaming for a new bike.*

The people in the team car are shaking and barely breathing. Tony doesn't get up. I struggle to internalize these scenes.

Five of seven riders were on the ground. They took quite a beating. Badly. I hope it's not fatal. Suddenly, I start having doubts about my red dress for Madrid.

No, no, no, chill out. Primož crashed hard into the wall. In a replay, it looked like the peloton exploded. Its parts, bikes, and riders were flying through the air in every direction. A few minutes later, the banner on the screen reads »Tony abandons!« He's on the ground, covered with blood. Horrific.

There's no room for sympathy. No time to feel the pain. No one cares who's in and who's out, who has a shoe missing, who has no bike, who's showing his bare buttocks, who's missing a piece of skin, who lost a tooth or two, and who the doctors will be able to patch up to make it to tomorrow's start. No one cares what will happen, who panicked, who's in pain, who will lose, or who will win. Cycling is a beautiful sport. But tough. And in moments like this, it's appallingly hard to watch.

In front, they're going full steam ahead. No one is waiting for the red jersey, even though it's one of the unwritten rules of professional cycling – you fight for the jersey on the bike, eye to eye. This gentlemen's agreement is losing its value.

We're standing on the last climb in front of the stone bridge and see them descending the colonnade of trees on the other side of the river before turning left over a bigger bridge and then left again onto the climb for the last kilometer. The swarm of the peloton is too indistinguishable to show its true colors. When it passes us by, Primož has an imprint of the wall on his left side. His spirit doesn't look to be broken. That was the only thing I was worried about. We'll get through the rest.

We can't move to get to the podium. A narrow strip of flow along the fence doesn't move, not forward, not backward, not into the Middle Ages, not to Madrid.

The parking lot with team busses is full of people. There are Slovenian flags in front of the black-and-yellow bus. He won't be coming, but I can't make myself tell them that.

We speak on the phone later. He doesn't say much, as always when he's hurt. " Why's this happening at the end and always on these fucking flat stages? And we were exactly where we were supposed to be." *Exhale.* " Shit, Tony was all covered in blood." *Because it's not over yet, I think to myself, but I rather bite my tongue.*

The fact that the team vehicle drove off with Primož after changing his bike, leaving their other rider, bloody, in the middle of the road, shows how rough and cruel this sport can be. Oh, go stuff yourselves! Who needs this?

"I half flew over the wall. I scratched both arms under my elbows and my hip. I hit the hip so hard I didn't feel my leg for a while. I wasn't sure I was going to be able to pedal." *I close my eyes and grind my teeth. »Just one more,« I say, »we'll get through one more.« Silence. »Won't we?« And then, he has to go.*

He leaves me to think. You always mull over why something happened. You're bargaining through your desires and wishes, stubbornly ignoring the signs screaming that it's enough already, obstinately rejecting the thought that this is how it has to be because the strongest carry the heaviest burdens. Inexplicable voices from nowhere scream ... I don't know what, I can't make it out. Hang on, don't let your dreams cruelly crash and burn.

»He stands tall, he fires back,« I hear on one of the replays. I won't let him crash and burn, not even against the wall. The unimaginable dimension of an imminent ending is a lesson. We are too close to the epilogue for it to be of any value. Two days; two days of attention, fixated on every meter of the road under the bike, and a fierce hope that a moment of weakness doesn't come. Not repeating mistakes is one of the vital features of his character. And this guy is utterly annoyed with himself if he's not winning.

We'll spend the night at the same spot as yesterday. When I scroll through the podium ceremony photos, I see Bahamontes himself presenting the red jersey to Primož. I was wrong to presume him dead at 92. He's as old as the hills, but he's still going strong. I'm interested in legends' history, and I like to take my hat off to those who deserve it. His life was littered with hardships. In a weird coincidence, I have the book of Max Leonard with me. He met Bahamontes a few years ago.

»The family was poor but the Spanish Civil War and the Franco regime lowered them, like many, into abject poverty. For a while his father broke rocks as a road-mender's mate; for two years, the 11-year-old Federico had to help him. As a teenager, Bahamontes stole stale bread and rotten fruit, and even killed cats to stave off his family's hunger (cats that, Alasdair Fotheringham writes, his mother gutted and stuffed and which the family called 'baby goats').

Riding a bike was part of this struggle to survive. By 18, Bahamontes was working as a market trader, unloading lorries and then picking out and selling all the rotten fruit the stallholders didn't want, and he saved the money he made to buy a bike.«
(Max Leonard, Higher Calling, page 110)

I confirm with overexaggerated nodding that the eagle of Toledo was one of the greatest. No argument there; the old man is indestructible. I'm thinking. About cats, among other things. Meanwhile, Lev doesn't want to sleep and is screaming at the top of his lungs. All three of us have to take turns at the stroller. These days he's the only one that's keeping me grounded. With his tiny figure and cosmic love, he unwittingly reminds me of what's really important. The Vuelta is only a race. But we are eternal. There's some kind of a colorful projection on the front of the castle above the rampart.

You get hit by a lot of injustice in your life. Everything I am, everything we two and all of us on the road and at its side are experiencing these days is a complicated correlation of suffering, sacrifice, and love and affection; and here bodily pain soon becomes more or less unavoidable. There's also an identical mentality somewhere in its background. It just hurts. And you're subject to it.

Bahamontes said you couldn't get over mountain passes without sacrifice. There are a lot of different kinds of pain. The ones that happen on walls are a lot harder to understand than those the riders take on willingly when pushing up the climb.

The projection on the castle stops, Lev stops roaring, and my skirt stops flapping about in the calm. Those who found themselves on the hard ground today are having very difficult moments now. When the adrenaline wears off and the heat drains out, the body starts to ache and the riders learn to their despair that they didn't just hit the parts of their bodies where the jerseys were ripped. Wounds start to fester, and bruises start changing color. They'll probably have them even after Madrid. Until they bedazzle us again, tackling the climbs, enduring somehow more pleasant pain. We only have to survive tomorrow.

STAGE TWENTY

SEPTEMBER 14, 2019

ARENAS DE SAN PEDRO ·······➤ PLATAFORMA DE GREDOS

190 KM, MOUNTAIN

MAGICAL: POGAČAR TAKES THE STAGE AND GETS ON THE PODIUM,
ROGLIČ ON THE BRINK OF VICTORY [...]

Tadej Pogačar won stage 20 in grand style and jumped up to third place overall,
while Primož Roglič successfully defended the red jersey and can already think
about cooling a bottle of champagne for a historical Sunday celebration in
Madrid. [...]

Roglič comfortably controlled his closest rivals Alejandro Valverde of Spain and
Nairo Quintana of Colombia in the background. [...]

In the general classification before the last Sunday stage from Fuenlabrada
to Madrid (106.6 km), Roglič has two minutes and 33 seconds of advantage on
Valverde. The 29-year can be denied this historic win in the 74th Tour of Spain
only by force majeure or an unpredictable incident. Pogačar is third (+2:55) and
has regained the white jersey for the best young rider. [...] (RTV MMC 2019š)

SLO	1. ROGLIČ, PRIMOŽ (JUMBO-VISMA)	80:18:54
ESP	2. VALVERDE, ALEJANDRO (MOVISTAR)	+2:33
SLO	3. POGAČAR, TADEJ (UAE TEAM EMIRATES)	+2:55

THE BROKEN SPELL

Plataforma de Gredos, the end of the world, literally, September 14, 2019

Sierra de Gredos is a national park, and its mascot is an ibex. It feels like an eternity since we left Toledo. Light rain is keeping us company on our drive over the mountain passes, and on one of the climbs remnants of an old Roman road run parallel to the road we are on. I can't imagine how people used to travel in the days of yore. I'm nervous, just like the weather.

When I think about it later, forcing myself to think about those decisive finishes one more time, I have a few flashes before my eyes and no big words.

How could I miss something so obvious? At last, I reach deep into my ebbing memory, or memories, actually. They sting, just as if I'd cut myself with the knife I was slicing an apple with and waded straight into the salty ocean.

Sirens wail on the horizon because big decisions are always made in the mountains. Big news, the twentieth stages are bad luck for Primož Roglič.

Restlessness reduces everything that I should remember in order to form some kind of a cogent thought. Fucking stage twenty. I can't even think of Monte Avena and Espelette. Or even Marseille, while we're at it.

But the spell revealed itself on the first try already. The first stage twenty was a nightmare. The finale of the Giro 2016 led the race into France – into the mountains, of course. After climbing Col de Vars, riders pressed on to Col de la Bonette with daunting 2751 meters; the French like to boast that it's the pass with the highest road in Europe, which is not entirely true. Nevertheless, they're prepared to argue with you about that, but that's not the point of this story. Having said that, I love Bonette. It's amazing.

The road slithered through endless rock fields, soft grasses that sheep graze to the roots during the summer, and dark walls of shale that reminds me of Erzberg, the iron mountain in Austria. There's also Camp des Fourches there, a desolate bucolic settlement where herdsmen howl at the wolves in harmony with their Pyrenean sheepdogs.

Then there were also Colle della Lombarda, with its disgusting incline on the top, Isola 2000, and Sant'Anna di Vinadio at the end, a short and therefore sweet, but even more terrifying road, that leads to the monastery.

But when we drove up to Isola in June 2018, Rogli didn't remember it, and he adamantly maintained he had never raced there. When it comes to his memory, his excuse is always a time trial; according to him it starts destroying his brain when he goes into the red zone, and his pulse reaches 185 bpm. Then, at the beginning of a dark and humid tunnel, it struck him. He threw his head back, saying: " Oh, right! Fuck, this was hard. Oh, yeah." And so on. He didn't win. He didn't even come close. But he inscribed his first Grand Tour on the list of finished races. And that's a special something.

The next year, the next Grand Tour, the Tour de France 2017. We barely managed to cool down from the heat under Galibier. The first Slovenian win in the Tour, his win, left me speechless in a weird floating state where everything was possible. And that win was mine, too. I was standing in the finish area for a reason but not aware that history was being written. The first will stay the first for eternity.

The Tour took a funny detour south, all the way to Marseilles, before ending in Paris. I managed to get there after six-hours long drive from the Alps (with Primož's agent) only to crash into a car parked in front of the hotel. Then I got stuck in the elevator because of a blackout. I nearly had a stroke because these things are always very unpleasant for me. Later that day, I was sitting on a small iron roof balcony in a negligee on what was a very hot July evening, looking down at the road, bustling with people. It seemed so French to me that I still remember that feeling. In the evening, we had fish in the old harbor where the warm July breeze waltzed among the heavy wooden sailboat masts swaying in the bay. It stinks, yes. It was exactly as I remembered from the last time I was here in January, some years ago, when our distant cousin Laurent married a general's daughter in the fortress above the harbor.

The next day, after wandering around the town and getting blistering sunburns on my back, it was time. Time to go to the magnificent Stade

Vélodrome, a stadium where the Olympique de Marseille play – but not that day. That day we were there to see kings of carbon bikes at the start and finish of an individual time trial. I don't know what the capacity of the stadium is, but it was the most powerful thing I have ever experienced. The stadium stirred into waves, even when Primož started.

As Mattia and I were following the race on the screen, the camera showed him; he stopped by the fence and was waiting to change the bike with the spare one from the car. The day ended there and then. I had the feeling that the stadium went quiet. A connector popped out of its gearbox and stopped working because the gears were electronic. Terminé, the end, done.

While driving from Marseilles to Paris to experience Champs-Élysées cycling style for the first time, I had a lot of time to turn things around in my head and sort them out. Instead, I only remembered that the guy stamping the tickets at the stadium was the same one I saw at the hotel reception.

The next penultimate stage is also from France, but one year later, on the Tour 2018, Espelette at the edge of Europe on the day when I fell into shit. The night before, we made camp in a Basque field, encircled with a wooden fence and full of mint covered in soft dew, the sort of mint destined for the literary glory.

We dreamt big and crashed hard. He was good, but not good enough to stay on the podium of the biggest race in the world. Contender number one in the Basque time trial that took us by surprise. It was the only time the Basque Country hurt us. The TV deemed the route The Roglič Profile. After the glorious day before, we might have just wanted too much.

He launched countless attacks on what was almost a circle of death over Tourmalet, Soulor, and Aubisque, but he only managed to peel himself away from the group on a descent through Eaux-Bonnes, a health resort town with thermal springs. Every bullet takes a toll; I know that. He came to Laruns alone. We got stuck on the last pass, on the top of Col d'Aubisque, caught in a game of Tetris with campers and the wild horses that were cramming themselves among them. Helicopters scared them, so they tried to find shelter.

For some intangible reason, we made fast and honest friends with the mountain lodge owner, a gray-mustachioed guy. With génépi, a green liqueur from French mountains, probably more from the Alps than from the Pyrenees, we celebrated a victory that really belongs there, on the

Tour de France 2018. A magical morning at the Aubisque mountain pass.

Aubisque. In cycling, magnificence rarely takes place anywhere else but in the mountains. And oh, what mountains!

It's true that he remained alone only later, but from the perspective of emotions, the triumph remains somewhere in the Pyrenees' heights. When

we were leaving, that petit monsieur with a typical Basque hat gazed upon us almost with tears in his eyes. He was standing by the window where I was clutching the steering wheel; I took Primož's hat off my head and left it as a souvenir. As a reminder of one of the hardest mountain stages' winner in the Tour ever. And his wife, who with insane speed backed the camper between a huge rock and his lodge while the clutch was burning and grass was flying from under the wheels, and all the Basque fans were frantically running around with bricks, scared I would knock down their bar. It makes sense to note here that they're very friendly and nice and in love with cycling. Only weeks later did it occur to me the little man reminded me of my dearly departed uncle Rudi from Marseilles.

But these three penultimate stages were nothing compared to the last twentieth.

A hot Saturday, as June has already started. Swollen legs and a belly with someone residing in it, making it so big that it obscured my view even when sitting on the couch. Lev, who was vigorously kicking under my heart, prevented me from going mad. Compared to this love, all the races are insignificant irrelevances.

The first twentieth in 2019. When we went to look at it in November 2018, a day after Mortirolo, and when I was alternately passing water bottles to Primož through the car window and vomiting, it was a sunny day and it didn't look that bad. Terribly difficult, yes, but horrifically torturous, no.

I was naïve and wrong to be scared of the stage's beginning with a monstrous Manghen Pass. True, he was already alone there, but on a long descent, the group of favorites was joined by others, among them his teammates. The real hell broke loose on the last climb.

We knew he would get a penalty because of his fan, but he started to fade on top of that. Our family was on the last climb with the camper, and I was in Ljubljana, petrified, shaking, and hyperventilating, almost going into labor. Friends were coming into my apartment during the stage, but I *greeted none of them; I didn't take my eyes off the screen, and I'm sorry for that. I had my hands cupped, breathing into them, eyes glued to the TV with only one thing in mind – for god's sake, hang in there!*

The higher the race goes, the more horrific it gets. Chinks are starting to appear in his armor. More and more. I hope I'm the only one seeing them, but I know it's not so. He's alone in no man's land, with one foot over the cliff and one hand still clenching the first Grand Tour podium in the history of the Slovenian nation. By the end of the day, it slips through his fingers. He falls off the throne.

It's like I'm being skinned alive. And him, too. All of a sudden, he's absolutely vulnerable, exposed even, and transient. More and more falling behind, he's almost irrelevant in the TV broadcast, but it's heartbreaking. Everyone attacked him, and even he attacked himself. My folks tell me he was as pale as death in the finish. He didn't even recognize them.

But I also noticed something else on the passes and by the road that day. Whole collections of Slovenian flags, a pilgrimage into the Dolomites that might as well have been a holy mountain chain. A cycling fan revolution and unrepeatable volleys as a tribute to Slovenian warriors. I was left speechless. It's impossible to get higher praise in sports.

It was like they were racing on the home ground and as if they united the Slovenian spirit in some kind of indescribable and incomprehensible emotion. And there is no need to worry that he might not have noticed it. In one of the rare instances of him putting his emotions into words, he admitted to me he had goosebumps at the starting line and that he almost teared up when he saw the Slovenian flags and heard his name.

You can rest assured that the presence of thousands of his fellow countrymen along the road helped a lot in preventing him from dropping dead.

For a short moment in the painful stage 20 of the Tour of Italy, we were all united in our pride of being Slovenian. Some on the climbs that the race scaled, and others on lounge chairs in front of their TVs.

When the Passion up the mountain ended, we drove off to Verona. To the last battle. At Postojna already, I started feeling pain in my lower back. Yeah, right, this is all I need now – contractions. No, you'll wait!

In the footage from the finish area, he was – I have no words. A pale shadow of himself, dignified and upstanding, but unrecognizable. At least there was one thing I was sure of; as long as he is breathing, he isn't thinking about abandoning.

I meet him in front of the hotel in the evening. Not as much meet as I wait for him, because I know I have to. He comes off the bus; we came to Verona almost at the same time. He's deflated and colorless.

The swanny tells me later he was lying on the bus floor covered with poultices all the way to the hotel. He doesn't want to have dinner; he has no appetite. No one on the team is in a good mood, and everyone is worried. It's only normal since they've been relentlessly attacking the road for the last 20 days, and they've been apart from their loved ones for about five days more. He's whining and complaining – which he never does.

I'm starting to worry, and rightly so, but I try my best not to be swept away. I desperately hold to my smile with my last claw, even though a cocktail of hormones, sadness, and helplessness, but most of all uncertainty and fear, about the next day almost pushes me underground. My neck is throbbing and the lump of my anxiety is getting so big that I fear it will shoot itself out of me and break a window on one of the cars in the parking lot where we're standing.

I'm not sure about tomorrow. I cry in the car. My two best friends are with me. My family is still descending from the pass. On a dirt parking lot not far from a curve of tomorrow's time trial, we wait for them until one in the morning. My legs get so swollen that they're thick like they were in a plaster cast up to my knees. And my due date is in one week. Why the hell do I need this? I hesitate. I fret. I have no idea.

I'm consoling myself thinking if I really burst here, my son will be named Giovanni. There are 60 million Italians; they have to be born somewhere. I don't know what will happen if Primož blows up. Oh, stop, for god's sake!

Stirring up painful memories invites fear, an unpleasant and indeterminate sort that repulses me and makes me wish I didn't exist. My anxiety would be so much lower if this were only stages 19 or 21. Will the spell of stage 20 finally be broken?

We're in the present now, in Ávila, Spain, where we're trying to reach the last climb. When we get there, people are frantically removing fences, flailing their arms, and trying to stuff us between a trash container and a row of busses. They don't care that we might close the road with our huge vehicle. Obviously, we're very late. Everyone knows us by now. We share similar dark circles under our eyes with the race staff. We're so late I only manage to get fully dressed outside.

The van is already running when we pack ourselves onto the rear seats. There's much too many of us, and we really need to hurry. There are four of us in the back and a baby in a shell. One of four has a meter-long camera. In front, people are sitting on the floor, one on top of one another: with all the breathing, the inside is soon as foggy as the outside. We crawl uphill at a snail's pace. It's fairly obvious there won't be any busses at the top today either. But it's nice because I won't need to argue in the front row for a change.

The landscape is northern and mossy, with a coniferous forest here and there, sharp green grass, and occasional rocks. Like Norway in the middle of August, even the rain falls just as softly as that summer, close to Trondheim.

There's nothing at the top. Even the shallow V-shaped valley ends, and there are no mountain trails. There is just one portable toilet and an inflatable tent for journalists.

The waiting line for the toilet takes half of the stage. I leave Lev with the cameraman, who has four kids, which is a consolation for me. All good. Everyone on top of the hill is shivering with cold. There are not many spectators, but I still see Slovenian flags. We mingle incognito among journalists in the tent– it's maybe a degree or two warmer there.

Just go on and try to throw me out if you dare. I'll bite through your tent so it deflates, I swear. Pogačar is attacking again, which I find fascinating. He's fighting to get back on the podium, but I'm more worried about what's happening behind him. It's not nearly over yet, and it's still the twentieth stage. I don't know, and I can't assess how he's feeling, even though he has glasses with clear lenses. His eyes are wide open, focused; he's not relieved yet. It's wet and dim, and maybe it's even raining a bit. I know we're in for a bloody fight and undoubtedly a stomach ulcer. Will we be able to say he won the Vuelta at the end of the day?

Tick-tock, tick-tock, tick-tock. I drew blood biting my lip, and I feel a lump under my sternum. I'm standing so stiffly, crossing my arms and hugging myself to stop shivering, that I'll surely get a cramp in my elbow. I don't even know if that is physically possible. When I hold Lev in my arms, though, I realize again that everything will be fine.

Under the point where the hill meets clouds' darkness, our raised national flags spontaneously form a proud trellis. Slovenian flags in Spanish mountains, almost at the end of the world, are something indescribably unbelievable. I wonder how this majestic experience happened to us and what did we do to deserve it.

He leaves the group and rolls alone over the finish line under the magnificent arch of this patriotic mission to the high outskirts of Madrid. He won one of the big three.

I'm relieved, and I transform from an angry, prickly porcupine into a soft and sweet panda. He doesn't show an ounce of joy, which saddens me a little bit.

I know he'll stubbornly maintain when they ask him about his win that it's not over because tomorrow there is another stage, and that we're not in Madrid yet. We're close, true, but not there yet. Party pooper. A real sourpuss. Or maybe he's just focused on his job? Only later does it occur to me that it's also about respecting his rivals. Bony guys on bikes, hovering between freezing and squeezing out a smile, are still riding to the top of the hill long after the race had finished for us.

I have to celebrate in secret. When he later awaits the media behind the table in the tent, where we spent the day, he's still sour. I know he's relieved and still very wounded from Toledo. While his icy majesty answers the media's questions monosyllabically, Lev squeaks in the corner. The

Spanish *Marca* would write the next day that he is the coldest champion in the history of the race and that even his son had a lot more to say than he did.

We descent from the mountain together in the van, which is an extreme honor. We sit in the back seat, quiet, each holding a non-alcoholic beer. We don't need to speak, our eyes speak a thousand words – we are celebrating the Vuelta.

That moment, when the sun was already blowing a kiss goodbye behind the hills and the landscape was flying by with the three of us in the back seat like a weird happy fellowship, is firmly imprinted in my memory. I doubt I have ever felt stronger love than then and there. I left the heavy stones I'd been carrying around for the past few weeks up there, with the ibexes. The twentieth disperses like dust in front of my eyes; it splinters like a tormenting mirage.

We hold hands over the sleeping cub. **"** We did it,**"** he says wordlessly with his face. »We did it,« I agree silently.

We go our separate ways to Madrid. Madrid, our distant longing before all this drama, is within our reach now, and we're almost at the doorstep. Primož's and my family will take off from Vienna any minute now. We'll all sleep in the same hotel. We in the camper in front of it, next to the airport. Planes were humming, and that night, above us, there was a starry sky.

STAGE TWENTY-ONE

SEPTEMBER 15, 2019

FUENLABRADA ········▶ MADRID

107 KM, FLAT

ROGLIČ'S HISTORIC WIN - THE EAGLE FROM ZASAVJE LANDED IN MADRID [...]

The cyclists finished the three weeks of hell in the Spanish loop. At the champions' parade in Madrid, Primož Roglič officially became the Vuelta winner, achieving one of the greatest successes in the history of Slovenian sports. Fabio Jakobsen took the last stage in the sprint.

The 29-year Roglič celebrated the first Slovenian win in three-week races. The Eagle from Zasavje had already made history earlier that year, when he became the first Slovenian to take the podium in a Grand Tour with third place in the Tour of Italy. This time he went a step further and took the red jersey as well as the green one for the best rider in the points classification.

The Slovenian celebration was complemented by Tadej Pogačar, who stepped on the podium in his debut. Slovenian cycling biggest hope won three stages and topped his success with the white jersey for the best young rider aged 25 or under. The polka dot jersey for the best climber was the only one that failed to end up on a Slovenian torso and was instead taken by Geoffrey Bouchard of France. [...]
(RTV MMC 2019t)

OFFICIAL GENERAL CLASSIFICATION OF LA VUELTA 2019

SLO	1. ROGLIČ, PRIMOŽ (JUMBO-VISMA)	83:07:14
ESP	2. VALVERDE, ALEJANDRO (MOVISTAR)	+2:33
SLO	3. POGAČAR, TADEJ (UAE TEAM EMIRATES)	+2:55

We got to the finish line. The Tour of Spain had ended. We came to Madrid, which we secretly glanced at every now and then in the back of the roadbook. But we'll have fun only when the race really ends. The last stages are usually reserved for celebration in Grand Tours, a sort of holiday parade after a long way home. Everyone at the start of the twenty-first can be damn proud of themselves.

In Spain, the last stage begins in late afternoon. The start wasn't in the city, but when the riders got to Madrid's center, the route circled it a few times. Closing laps in famous city centers are typical for big races and contribute to the excitement, even though the unwritten rule states that only sprinters race on the last day. Jersey holders toast with champagne for photographers while spinning their pedals and riding around famous squares and monuments. In Vuelta 2019, they were toasting with beer.

The legendary Paris laps around the Louvre, the Arc de Triomphe, and the Champs-Élysées at the end of the Tour de France are accompanied by jet planes drawing the French flag across the sky in colored smoke. The tradition of the Paris finish goes back to 1975. The French are masters of spectacle, while Italians love to play around with different versions of concluding stages.

The team

Even though it was equally spectacular, the Tour of Italy 2019 didn't end with laps as it had many times before in Milan, Turin, and other cities. It ended rather with an individual time trial that finished in Arena di Verona. A while ago, the ITT was held in Milan, and surely in other places through the years. A modern gladiatorial spectacle in all its glory. Such stages differ from laps not only in profile but also in the fact that, usually, nothing happens in GC in those laps, while the ITT can change the ranking at the top considerably, especially if the time differences are small; in this case, the race really doesn't end until the last meter.

PARC DES PRINCES

FOOTBALL LOVERS WILL BE DELIGHTED WITH THIS SHOUTOUT. THE FOOTBALL GIANT PSG'S HOME STADIUM WAS THE *NATIONAL STADIUM OF FRANCE* UP TO 1998, WHEN IT WAS DISPLACED BY THE *STADE DE FRANCE*. BUT ITS BEGINNINGS WERE NOT CONNECTED TO FOOTBALL AT ALL. AT FIRST, IT WAS A VELODROME, BUILT IN 1897, AND THE TOUR DE FRANCE'S LAST STOP FROM 1903 TO 1967.

NO WONDER, IF YOU THINK THAT HENRI DESGRANGE MANAGED THE VELODROME. WE ALREADY TOUCHED ON HIS ROLE IN CYCLING.

ITS NAME, THE PARK OF PRINCES, DERIVES FROM THE 18TH CENTURY WHEN THE AREA WHERE THE STADIUM STANDS TODAY WAS A ROYAL HUNTING GROUND.

If you're not a fervent fan of Spaniard Mikel Landa, stage 21 of the Giro 2019, where Primož attacked the first GC podium in Slovenian history, was very intense.

But that is by no means the most brutal story the last day of a race can offer. The Tour de France 1989 ended with a time trial in Paris. The organizers were obviously a tad flexible then. But just a tad. The finish of the individual time trial was, much like now, on the Champs-Élysées.

Frenchman Laurent Fignon came into the last stage as the general classification leader with a 50-second advantage over the young American Greg LeMond. In what was one of the most dramatic finales, LeMond won that Tour by eight seconds, which is still the smallest winning time difference in history. He performed magnificently with an average speed of more than 54 km/h, favoring also from improved aerodynamic components; don't forget that LeMond rode with a helmet, time trial handlebars, much like these we see on time trial bikes today, and disc wheels, while Fignon rode a classic road bike. If today's aerodynamics experts are to be believed,

Fignon would have won that Tour even if he had only put a hat on his head. I don't know how much you know about his hairstyle, but it was every bit as interesting as this story.

And if we stick to things that riders definitely should have on their heads – helmets have only been mandatory in races since 2003. This safety measure was taken seriously only after Kazakh Andrey Kivilev had a fatal accident in the Paris–Nice race, and doctors later established that a helmet would have probably saved his life.

Let's round this story off and go back to laps in Madrid. Per gentlemen's agreement, no one attacks the leader's jersey the last day. To put it simply, the general classification stays the same as after the stage the day before. Real racing in the last stage begins when riders finish the first lap around the city. In the group of riders, who look like they're on a leisurely Sunday ride, suddenly all hell breaks loose. Attacks, formations, attempts, looking for domestiques, forming breakaways, utter chaos.

The Vuelta's farewell in Madrid

WHO'S WHO?

IF YOU'RE WATCHING THE CHAMPIONS' PARADE, OH, PARDON ME, STAGE 21 OF THE VUELTA IN MADRID, YOU MIGHT GOT CONFUSED ABOUT WINNERS' JERSEYS AND WHO WEARS THEM. SO LET ME EXPLAIN WHO'S WHO IN THIS CONUNDRUM.

IN THE LAST STAGE OF THE TOUR OF SPAIN, THE GREEN JERSEY WAS WORN BY COLUMBIAN NAIRO QUINTANA, THE FIFTH IN THE GENERAL CLASSIFICATION. IS THERE A JERSEY FOR THE FIFTH RIDER? NO. HE WORE IT BECAUSE THE FIRST IN THE POINTS CLASSIFICATION FOR THE GREEN JERSEY PRIMOŽ ROGLIČ WORE THE RED JERSEY OF THE GENERAL CLASSIFICATION WINNER, AND THE SECOND IN GC TADEJ POGAČAR WORE THE WHITE JERSEY FOR THE BEST YOUNG RIDER, THE THIRD IN THE POINTS CLASSIFICATION ALEJANDRO VALVERDE WORE THE WORLD CHAMPION'S JERSEY, AND THE FOURTH IN THE GREEN JERSEY CLASSIFICATION SAM BENNETT WORE THE IRISH NATIONAL CHAMPION'S JERSEY. EASY AS PIE.

When the bell marks the beginning of the last lap, a swarm of bees in different jerseys frantically lunges ahead, pushing as hard as they can. It's a sprint like any other, only with a slightly bigger relief at the end, because this really *is* the end. For some time, anyway.

A magnificent ceremony follows, an especially solemn event in Grand Tours. The announcement of the best in the Tour of Spain 2019 was held in front of a striking fountain and palace at Plaza de les Cibeles in Madrid, intended only for heroes. Football club Real Madrid celebrates there with their fans.

ZDRAVLJICA IN MADRID

Madrid, September 15, 2019

If I had started the last chapter with »we came to an end«, I'd have to knock myself over the head because I hate clichés. But we did.

I'm not thinking about that when I wake up by the Madrid airport. Its buzz is now very familiar to me. I'm thinking about what to wear. I'm thinking that Lev, my little mouse, will be three months old in a few days and that I still have a pregnancy line on my belly. I'm thinking about how many times I'm going to cry today.

The Vuelta is proverbially a hilly race, won by climbing specialists. Yeah, right! The Vuelta is one of the biggest races in the world, won by the biggest whackos with a constantly ripped jersey, who are not prepared to bow to anyone and anything, and who have massive, iron balls.

I'm sleepless, of course. The best way to describe my state would be to say I feel like a flattened piece of shit. I don't know if I should relax, show restrained joy, contain my sharpness, be diplomatically cool, or just be euphorically wild. Where's the manual on how to behave when you win the first Grand Tour in the history of your country?

Madrid is closed. They'll start in Fuenlabrada, not far from the capital, and then circle its center nine times before bringing this year's Vuelta to an end. The lap blocks almost the whole city center, and those on the inside will stay there at least until the race workers, who await the end as anxiously as we do, set them free. The only open store is a Chinese one. I unsuccessfully look for champagne to celebrate the sensationally spectacular result. I screwed up royally – again. In the end, I find it in a bakery.

The stage starts, and before they come into the city the first time, I look up in vain to find the jets flying over our heads. They won't come, I conclude exactly when people start to hustle by the fence, anxiously looking at the timeline where it says the riders should be here any minute now.

It's impossible to miss their arrival. A swarm of police motorcycles with lights and sirens, a humming helicopter that pushes the air down, so we feel it in our hair, and then in the distance them, coming into the flat.

A peculiar, homogenous formation of heroes, each of them an enclave in itself, but everyone dependent on one another, moving like one. The flickering heat gusts up from the asphalt in front of them, fogging up their magnificent arrival like in American movies set in the desert, but instead

of cars, we see the sunburnt legs of the peloton coming closer, moving up and down like pistons, full of scars and scabs and countless kilometers indelibly imprinted in their weary and exhausted muscles. And the pain, of course. They know they don't have to go far now.

Their ride is fairly calm, but as they come in a pack, the ground trembles from fans cheering, and if someone walked into their way, they'd simply mince and digest them like in the Lion King cartoon, if you remember the

scene where the wild thumping of bison herd announces that there's no return.

The peloton rides by, tightly packed and exuberant, not too fast, but fast enough for you to feel you have to step back because the force preceding it pushes you away from the fence. Even its sound is alluring, once you accept it as a part of the machinery. Prancing on pedals fizzles its solo, which comes in a very steady rhythm, probably because the bicycles of the best riders in the world are as well maintained as the violins of the best virtuosos.

They run as smoothly as an uninterrupted zzz, relentlessly cut through with the boisterous cheering of everyone who came to pay them tribute. The helicopter is merely playing a backup. Swoosh, the hollow grumble dies down, they're gone in a second, and then we have some time to catch a breath until their next arrival.

I was just standing there, about a meter from the fence, like a statue, not even clapping. My silence was deafening; I couldn't utter a peep, shame on me. I just felt like my whole facade was about to crack open. I tried to control my sobbing, but the more I wanted to stifle it, the more it kept bursting out when it was the last thing I needed. The consciousness of the infinity of the moment I was in struck me only for a short instance in that victory lap. It will stay forever, and not only in my memory.

Inhale, exhale, blink; I can't unravel the cluster in my throat, and the lump that twirled and accumulated through the whole year is still there. It comes when the intensity eases up a bit. Things I will remember, things I will forget, hormonal imbalances, existential distress, the best moments in my life, and the deepest fallacies, the stress, the joy, surprises, and pains.

Even now, my flaw of going back to the past doesn't let me down. I feel a premonition of sinking into a place where I'll relive everything. The reflection glows in a pink hue at first, as expected. But only for a moment. I got over the Giro, at least I think so. But the unforgettable heartache incessantly rocks my purpose.

Sunday, Arena di Verona, Italy. The first weekend in June. It's boiling hot, and 45 rows of chairs that were once made of marble in the oval of the arena are filled with all the colors of cycling world. I ignore the signs of labor – something else is more important now. A few seconds. I won't talk about the before and after; because it's too much, because I don't remember, because there is no night, because the whole day is crammed into those three minutes, we shivered with fear whether it would be enough.

Never in my life have I felt so out of control, even if I wanted something that was irreparably out of my reach. I tried so hard with a swollen face and a mighty sunstroke to play it cool and elegant, or at least not to faint with three cameras under my nose. My protector Vinko blows a gasket a few times while I frantically run in every possible direction like an insane goat and says something like: »Where are you going with that big belly of yours?« I don't know what or who to ask for help in my thoughts. Maybe the universe? I don't know where to go or what to do. Vinko turns out to be a bodyguard of pregnant lunatic sisters and holds the black and yellow umbrella above my head to make some shadow so my kid doesn't roast inside me, and so I'm possibly left with a living brain cell or two. The latter didn't necessarily work.

The fact that a woman in some other team's clothing walked up to me, took my hands, and very confidently said that everything would be all okay says everything about how shaken I looked. The 24 hours before that moment were the most horrible in his career and our relationship. If his face was the color of ash in previous stages, it was the color of granite in that one and that hurt. When I look upon the stands full of fans, I see patches of Slovenian flags. I feel they're also there to support me; among them are some of my dearest friends.

I wish so badly he would succeed. So much so, I almost don't think about myself. We dreamt the same dream, and with a silent agreement, we set a goal to get to Verona. And after that, we would be together, and together we can achieve anything. I have to scrape up a lot of strength to show him I didn't stop believing.

If a guy who doesn't flinch when he suffers a shoulder dislocation or has his finger stitched after a stage says that he can't walk and they have to bring him food to his bed before the most important moment of his career, you have good reason to worry. If, on top of that, you're very pregnant, well, actually, you should have given birth by now, and you're a hormonal wreck, your anxiety triples. Anyway, the difference between the third and the fourth place is in single digits, but standing on the podium or off it is a nuance that is almost definitely fateful and can profoundly change your life.

While we are shaking like the centrifuge in a washing machine for short, seconds-long moments, he makes it.

The relief is palpable, and the third place feels like a victory – for him and for me. I became so tired all of a sudden that I didn't know how to move my feet. He was even more exhausted. His comment probably doesn't belong in this undulating thread of my sentimental story. But when asked how he felt, not by journalists but by me, which was very disrespectful and out of place at that moment, he grumbled: **❝** Like a cat that's been run over and scraped off the road.**❞**

I leave the arena, sprinkled with pink confetti, with a merry heart and heavy legs. Astonishingly, I'm not thinking about gladiators, heroic feats, or lost lives. Primož leaves with the team.

I am thanking the arena in my own way. It was good to us; well either it was the arena, or maybe the Roman gods were. My head is full of the Italian canzoni we had been listening to non-stop for more than a month, just to adapt to the system. In half a year, I would be wondering why my little son calms down immediately when he hears the song Ti amo. There is something about arenas that make people talk about them for a long time after.

I'm thinking about how everything would be different now, and not just because of the podium. There's a stand with food and drink in the park, but they've run out of everything. We buy all of the French fries they had left. In the background, we hear parroting chants: »Co-lom-bi-a!«

We should be celebrating, but we're both too tired, and in the middle of the night in a wonderful hotel with a beautiful atrium and wooden ceilings, I suddenly sense he's not there. I find him in a tub, full of icy water, in strange pain and almost with tears in his eyes. It's four in the morning.

Then, we became a trio, and when the force of life showed like never before what is really important, he slowly began to come back. From the old husk, a new Primož emerged, healed, with a new motive and a clear vision. Anxious and with difficulty, he watched the Tour de France from the sofa. It was a too long and too hot July evening, and the baby was still almost glued to my body when I accidentally clicked something on the computer, and it was there.

Intentional, or maybe not, a hint I only managed to figure out from the silhouette of some other profiles after the next few sleepless nights, when the day was already rising around our local hiking spot, the Mount Saint Mary. We're going for the Vuelta. It dawned on me some morning, and I didn't even have to ask to get his confirmation. I was ecstatic, of course.

Third place is not the pedestal he wanted to climb on; that was immediately clear to me. Because if you have only a one-dimensional notion about sports, that kind of comparison isn't very acceptable, leading to quite a clash in comprehension. He's always the best rider for me, but as far as he's concerned, he's only the best when winning – and he always could win better. There's no upper limit.

The spirit of a champion, and he's definitely one of them, is a special thing you either have or you don't, and it's much more than just a metaphor. When you were in second grade, did you time yourself with a watch, how fast you run from the bus stop to your home, every single day, even if you lived on a steep hill that Italians would immediately describe as Muro? No? Neither did I.

For someone who is »ordinary«, the glittery capability of the chosen and undoubtedly best ones may also be a burden in the everyday mediocrity, which sometimes comes to light in banality of unsuccessful attempts that are merely a minor lesson within a larger story. And the Vuelta was not that. We excluded ordinary from our repertoire a long time ago.

The colossal blindness of the first, which befalls to him by his name itself; the spectrum of possibilities is endless – because once he starts pushing the pedals he's unmistakably tough. The first maglia rosa, *the first Grand Tour podium, the first triple[48], the first with a Tour de France stage win, the first Slovenian who is number one in the UCI World Rankings, the first with a Grand Tour under his belt. It's a long list of triumphs.*

I wake up only when the bell loudly announces the last, ninth lap. Little Lev is nice and kind as if he knew how he should handle his mother on this stressful day. He's wearing the Vuelta T-shirt, fully covering his tiny legs, and avidly playing with the tail of a stuffed bull, so his mouth is full of red hair. He doesn't care that he's under a loudspeaker, he doesn't care they're ringing bells like in a cathedral, and he doesn't care the history is being written. My sweet little Lev, the whole world will be your home.

The last lap brings a general joyful panic. The excitement is comparable to the New Year's countdown. Everyone we love the most is there. The speed is much faster than the first time, so much so that we only see the riders' backs when they swoosh by us. Who's seen him? Has anyone seen him? Everyone nods, and that calms me down.

And then it hits me: in a few moments, a certain dream will be realized, and with it, many other dreams. When the sprint trains start falling apart, when the domestiques have done their job in the Vuelta for the last time and are happily letting the peloton go to enjoy the adoration of the masses for a few moments more. When team cars in the back honk excitedly and sprinters fervently fight for the best position in the last 500 meters, something else is happening at the rear of the peloton, where you don't usually see the winner's jersey.

---

[48] I. e. the first Slovenian with stage wins in all three Grand Tours.

With the team that stood firmly behind him and had his back when needed, they try to hold one another over their shoulders for a historical photograph. Relief and finally a much-anticipated smile when they try to align and ride over the finish line. The clock stops, cameras flashing like spotlights in a rave party. He won the Vuelta, and I'm crying at every word I want to say.

Calling over the radio giving thanks, maybe a swear word here or there, and most importantly, the awareness they have made it. »We are breathing again, thanks a lot,« I think to myself, but there's no Houston for me to send the message.

The race wasn't won here and now. It was won with all of the Giro's injustices, all the pain from memories, and lucky crashes that could have easily ended in tragedy. It was won with an unbreakable will, where he didn't think about quitting even for a split second, even though the whole world was wondering why he wasn't doing something less painful.

The reality only hits me full force when I see two Slovenian flags waving in the Spanish capital's most famous square. I aimlessly follow a fluorescent guy that's making way for us through the crowd so we can come as near to the podium as possible.

That podium will have a special place in Slovenian history. In front of the red marble-clad building behind the fountain, supposedly a palace, I try to soak up the moment. Not before, not later, now. For the first time, once and for all. The Slovenian anthem Zdravljica plays loudly, and I'm looking for Slovenian flags in the crowd. We're everywhere.

In the cycling religion, the jersey is the deity. A security guard is pushing him through the crowd as if he were a superstar. He's greeting people, and cameras follow him, flashes, and excited fans. It's hard to understand the happening and objectively internalize what just occurred. I'm too close to be aware of the magnificence of his achievement, his feat, and of the man himself.

The red lights are illuminating the evening sky and tired guys are loading the trucks with fences for the last time this year. We celebrate quietly, and I try to squeeze my bursting emotions into the solitude for a few moments more. I just want to hug him, over all these people, but I can't reach him. Instead of him, I hug our little bundle of joy and the rest of our dear ones.

In front of the camper immersed into the darkness, surrounded with shrieky Spanish, we share the moment we won the Tour of Spain. It will be eternal.

Every era celebrates its heroes. This era celebrates mine, and I'm immensely proud. But the obsession with winning avoided me for some reason, so the wins are of secondary meaning to me. Besides the fact that he suffers such dignified defeats, which sometimes aren't so much defeats as they are lessons for the future so he remains relentless, the most important thing to me is that he always returns to me safe and sound.

When you count stages in scabs and bruises and dinners you can't eat. When you fly over a wall, but you nevertheless act like the best actor in Hollywood that you're okay, and then keep trying and trying to no avail, that's when you pave your path to the stars.

When the Vuelta slowly starts to fade into a distant memory, and the snow on high mountain passes melts, we'll be waiting anxiously with them for new chances, we will watch again how they're killing each other on climbs. Fans, and maybe we'll be among them, too, will be in ecstasy and, yearning for the forbidden, they'll try to run in front of them.

And we, who will share the road with them again, will proudly cheer on anyone fighting their battle on the asphalt – champions, winners,

Our dearest

underdogs, and those in a gruppetto. We'll weave especially proud and inspiring feelings for those particularly dear to us.

Because with the peaks taken and finish lines behind us, there's only emptiness left and it is calling for new challenges. Wounds get healed, roads get forgotten, but the memories keep the nobility of joy for those beautiful days that have already past.

With affection for the suffering, I'm looking forward to everything new – roads, climbs, finishes, and memories. Cycling horizons are infinite, and the expanses are inviting and unexplored. One from the list, the red one, is ticked off.

A new morning rises over the control tower of the Madrid airport. It's an ordinary September Monday. Everyone quickly dispersed to different parts of the world. It's quiet, and there's no rush. Lev is the superstar of his own movie, as usual.

It isn't easy to put the awareness of achievement into the right place when you're emotional.

" A jersey is just a jersey," says the red specimen, whom the Dutch are filming for a documentary, but I know it's not quite like that. He stubbornly persists in proving himself. Oh, you, my communication train wreck.

»Come on, don't be like that,« I meow nonsensically because I fear I'm going to cry. It's silly but relentless, as if I were cutting onions all the time. I probably could have said something smarter.

Watching road cycling races can be very moving if you're a crybaby like me. Feelings possess you in every direction. You cry, and you laugh; they change how you envision holidays, and they push aside comfort for something much more explosive. Otherwise, why would millions roam to the Dolomites, the Alps, the Pyrenees, and other splendidly desolate mountain ranges instead of going to the beach? And no less in barely drivable campers, where incessantly stomping on the clutch turns into an ankle cramp? Not to mention the absence of electricity and the rare privilege of shower.

The winning and pain, the explosion, and the euphoria you experience as a fan, everything is somewhere out there. All of the passionate inclinations complement the whole picture of the involvement. We're a clan, a clan by the road. And sometimes, just a simple love draws us back there. The love of cycling or of a certain rider, take your pick.

I can't wait for us to return to some damn mountain.

And the red dress will be hanging in my closet, ready for one of the next times.

Hasta luego.

REFERENCES

- Leonard, Max. 2018. Higher Calling: Cycling's Obsession with Mountains. Pegasus Books.

- RTV MMC (2019a, Avgust 24) Saj ni res, pa je: Rogliču uvodno etapo pokvarila voda iz napihljivega bazena. Available at: https://www.rtvslo.si/sport/kolesarstvo/dirka-po-spaniji/saj-ni-res-pa-je-roglicu-uvodno-etapo-pokvarila-voda-iz-napihljivega-bazena/497714

- RTV MMC (2019b, Avgust 25) Roglič ekspresno nadoknadil izgubljen čas – Quintana dobil drugo etapo. Available at: https://www.rtvslo.si/sport/kolesarstvo/roglic-ekspresno-nadoknadil-izgubljen-cas-quintana-dobil-drugo-etapo/497782

- RTV MMC (2019c, Avgust 26) Mezgec tretji na Vuelti: „Boril sem se lahko le za drobtinice". Available at: https://www.rtvslo.si/sport/kolesarstvo/dirka-po-spaniji/mezgec-tretji-na-vuelti-boril-sem-se-lahko-le-za-drobtinice/497835

- RTV MMC (2019č, Avgust 27) Zmaga mladega Jakobsena, Mezgec četrti; odstopil Rogličev kolega Kruijswijk. Available at:https://www.rtvslo.si/sport/kolesarstvo/zmaga-mladega-jakobsena-mezgec-cetrti-odstopil-roglicev-kolega-kruijswijk/497923

- RTV MMC (2019d, Avgust 28) Lopez znova v rdeči majici, Roglič že drugi! Available at: https://www.rtvslo.si/sport/kolesarstvo/dirka-po-spaniji/lopez-znova-v-rdeci-majici-roglic-ze-drugi/498007

- RTV MMC (2019e, Avgust 29) Pogačar napadel v skupini favoritov, Uran in Roche odstopila. Available at: https://www.rtvslo.si/sport/kolesarstvo/dirka-po-spaniji/pogacar-napadel-v-skupini-favoritov-uran-in-roche-odstopila/498077

- RTV MMC (2019f, Avgust 30) Na vrhu sladkega pekla pred Rogličem le svetovni prvak. Available at: https://www.rtvslo.si/sport/kolesarstvo/dirka-po-spaniji/na-vrhu-sladkega-pekla-pred-roglicem-le-svetovni-prvak/498189

- RTV MMC (2019g, Avgust 31) Arndt imel največ moči med ubežniki v dežju - Edet prevzel rdečo majico. Available at: https://www.rtvslo.si/sport/kolesarstvo/dirka-po-spaniji/arndt-imel-najvec-moci-med-ubezniki-v-dezju-edet-prevzel-rdeco-majico/498285

- RTV MMC (2019h, September 1) Izjemni Pogačar dobil kraljevsko etapo v Andori, Roglič postavil rdeče temelje. Available at: https://www.rtvslo.si/sport/kolesarstvo/dirka-po-spaniji/izjemni-pogacar-dobil-kraljevsko-etapo-v-andori-roglic-postavil-rdece-temelje/498345

- RTV MMC (2019i, September 3) Matador Roglič pometel s konkurenco in oblekel rdečo majico. Available at: https://www.rtvslo.si/sport/kolesarstvo/dirka-po-spaniji/matador-roglic-pometel-s-konkurenco-in-oblekel-rdeco-majico/498432

- RTV MMC (2019j, September 4) Iturria z izjemnim pobegom do prve zmage v kariere. Available at: https://www.rtvslo.si/sport/kolesarstvo/dirka-po-spaniji/bask-iturria-z-izjemnim-pobegom-do-prve-zmage-v-karieri/498600

- RTV MMC (2019k, September 5) Zmaga Gilberta, Roglič in Pogačar v potrditev uspešnega dne udarila s pestmi. Available at: https://www.rtvslo.si/sport/kolesarstvo/dirka-po-spaniji/zmaga-gilberta-roglic-in-pogacar-v-potrditev-uspesnega-dne-udarila-s-pestmi/498706
- RTV MMC (2019l, September 6) Pogačar in Roglič v peklu Los Machucosa scvrla favorite. Available at: https://www.rtvslo.si/sport/kolesarstvo/dirka-po-spaniji/pogacar-in-roglic-v-peklu-los-machucosa-scvrla-favorite/498809
- RTV MMC (2019m, September 7) Bennett dobil sprint, Mezgec utrpel zlom črevnice. Available at: https://www.rtvslo.si/sport/kolesarstvo/dirka-po-spaniji/bennett-dobil-sprint-mezgec-utrpel-zlom-crevnice/498897
- RTV MMC (2019n, September 8) Roglič in Valverde s skupnimi močmi pobegnila ostalim favoritom. Available at: https://www.rtvslo.si/sport/kolesarstvo/dirka-po-spaniji/roglic-in-valverde-s-skupnimi-mocmi-pobegnila-ostalim-favoritom/498967
- RTV MMC (2019o, September 9) Fuglsangu prvič etapa Grand Toura, Roglič še bolj ušel Valverdeju. Available at: https://www.rtvslo.si/sport/kolesarstvo/dirka-po-spaniji/fuglsangu-prvic-etapa-grand-toura-roglic-se-bolj-usel-valverdeju/499024
- RTV MMC (2019p, September 11) Roglič preživel napad Quintane, Pogačar izgubil mesto. Available at:https://www.rtvslo.si/sport/kolesarstvo/dirka-po-spaniji/roglic-prezivel-napad-quintane-pogacar-izgubil-mesto/499235
- RTV MMC (2019r, September 12) Roglič v 18. etapi zaostal le za Higuito, Pogačar predal belo majico Lopezu. Available at: https://www.rtvslo.si/sport/kolesarstvo/dirka-po-spaniji/roglic-v-18-etapi-zaostal-le-za-higuito-pogacar-predal-belo-majico-lopezu/499301
- RTV MMC (2019s, September 13) Roglič padel in trpel, a na koncu vse „pod kontrolo". Available at: https://www.rtvslo.si/sport/kolesarstvo/dirka-po-spaniji/roglic-padel-in-trpel-a-na-koncu-vse-pod-kontrolo/499445
- RTV MMC (2019š, September 14) Pravljično: Pogačarju etapa in oder, Roglič pred skupno zmago. Available at: https://www.rtvslo.si/sport/kolesarstvo/dirka-po-spaniji/pravljicno-pogacarju-etapa-in-oder-roglic-pred-skupno-zmago/499538
- RTV MMC (2019t, September 15) Zgodovinska zmaga Rogliča – zasavski orel pristal v Madridu. Available at: https://www.rtvslo.si/sport/kolesarstvo/dirka-po-spaniji/zgodovinska-zmaga-roglica-zasavski-orel-pristal-v-madridu/499590
- Velopeloton, 2014. The circle of Death. Available at: https://velopeloton.com/circle-death/

KILOMETER ZERO

First published in Slovene in 2020 as Kilometer Nič
by Ariom Leone

Copyright © Lora Klinc 2020

The right of Lora Klinc to be identified as the author of this work has been asserted
in accordance with Sections 77 and 78 of the Copyright, Designs and Patents Act 1988.

© **Photographs** • Team Jumbo-Visma, Bettini Photo, Lora Klinc
Translation • Jolanda Blokar
Design • Atelje Globočnik
Editor • Mina Mušinović for Pipin's Book Ltd, Scotland
Printed in Slovenia by Trajanus d.o.o., Kranj
For UK • Pipin's Book Ltd, Muchalls, Scotland, www.pipins-book.co.uk

© 2021 Ariom Leone, d. o. o., Hoče, Slovenia

All rights reserved. No part of this publication may be reprinted, reproduced, stored
in a retrieval system, or transmitted, in any form or by any means, electronic, mechanical,
photocopying, recording or otherwise, without prior permission in writing of the publisher.

ISBN 978-0-9956314-4-1
A CIP catalogue record of this book is available from the British Library.